Who – What – When – Where – How – Why – MADE EASY

A NEW YORK TIMES BOOK

Who–What–When–Where–How–Why MADE EASY

A GUIDE TO THE PRACTICAL USE OF REFERENCE BOOKS

By Mona McCormick

QUADRANGLE BOOKS

For Ben

PERMISSIONS

The author wishes to thank the following publishers for their kind permission to quote from works held in copyright:

Chases' Calender Of Annual Events published by Apple Tree Press, Box 1012, Flint, Michigan.

Documents Of American History by Henry Steele Commager, published by Appleton-Century-Crofts, copyright 1963.

The Encyclopedia Of Sports by Frank G. Menke, published by A. S. Barnes, copyright 1968.

The American Heritage Dictionary Of The English Language © copyright 1969, 1970 by American Heritage Publishing Co., Inc.

Book Review Digest published by The H. W. Wilson Company, copyright 1905–date.

The New American Guide To Colleges by Gene R. Hawes, Columbia University Press, New York, copyright 1966.

The Encyclopedia Of American Facts and Dates edited by Gorton Carruth, published by Thomas Y. Crowell Company, Inc. New York, copyright © 1966.

Bulfinch's Mythology, revised edition, by Thomas Bulfinch, published by Thomas Y. Crowell Company, Inc. New York, copyright 1962.

Current Biography published by The H. W. Wilson Company, New York.

Asimov's Biographical Encyclopedia Of Science and Technology by Isaac Asimov, copyright © 1964 by Isaac Asimov, reprinted by permission of Doubleday & Company.

Folksingers and Folksongs In America by Ray M. Lawless, © copyright 1964 by Ray M. Lawless, published by Duell, Sloan & Pearce.

Editor & Publisher Market Guide by permission of the Editor & Publisher Market Guide, 1970 Edition.

Funk & Wagnalls New Standard ® Dictionary Of The English Language copyright 1969 by Funk & Wagnalls, A Division Of Reader's Digest Books, Inc.

A Practical Guide To Yoga by James Hewitt, published by Funk and Wagnalls, copyright 1968.

"The Member Of The Wedding" by *Cycopedia Of Literary Characters* edited by Frank N. Magill, copyright © 1963 by Salem Press, Inc. Reprinted by permission of Harper & Row, Publishers, Inc.

"I and Thou" from *Masterpieces of World Philosophy In Summary Form* edited by Frank N. Magill, copyright ©

CONTENTS

CONTENTS

PART III

FINDING AND USING REFERENCE BOOKS

INTRODUCTION

Listen, a terrible thing is happening. Today there is such a flood of printed material that students and readers are easily confused about where to begin and how to conduct a search for information.

Though intended primarily for students, this guide is also meant to aid general readers in their search for information. The purpose here is to offer an introduction to basic reference sources.

This is not, therefore, a comprehensive list of all good books in various fields. But, with an understanding of the basic books and procedures described here, a reader should be able to extend his search beyond the scope of this work. For *Who . . . What . . . When . . . Where . . . How . . . Why . . . Made Easy,* in addition to listing basic sources, is designed to indicate the wide range of material available. The bibliography on page 185 is included as a suggestion for further reading.

The method of this guide is to give an inkling or sample of the kind of information found in various sources. Descriptions will not dwell on the technical arrangement because that is best learned when a reader has the book in hand and has a motive for using it. Emphasis and treatment for each work vary according to probable use by the student. Full bibliographic information in Part I is given at the end of each chapter so the discussion is not interrupted. In Part II it is given with the annotation.

The pressures on today's students are phenomenal. The more familiar a student becomes with the methods of finding information, the easier it is for him to accomplish his goal. The hope is that this guide will remove at least some of the confusion created by the mushrooming literature of information.

PART I

Reference Books By Type

ALMANACS AND ATLASES

BIOGRAPHY

DICTIONARIES

ENCYCLOPEDIAS

NEWSPAPERS AND MAGAZINES

ALMANACS AND ATLASES

Almanacs are an old information source. The early ones were often produced by astrologers because a belief in the influence of the stars on human behavior, a desire to know the future, and superstition created a popular demand for prophecy.

In the beginning almanacs predicted, in addition to the daily weather, such catastrophes as fires, famine and plague. The editors faced the occupational hazards of being burned at the stake as sorcerers if they were right too often, or of losing their reputations if they were too often wrong. So they resorted to ambiguous language. An almanac in 1580 predicted: "The Sommer and Autumne shall sometyme encline unto driness, sometyme unto moysture: so the winter shall be partlye rough and partlye milde." In other words, a nice day unless it isn't.

The first printed American almanac was *An Almanack for New England for the Year 1639*, compiled by William Pierce. In 1733, Benjamin Franklin launched *Poor Richard's Almanack*, which became famous for the proverbs used to fill little spaces that occurred between the calendar days. Famous Franklin adages which appeared in his almanack are:

> Make haste slowly.
> Three may keep a secret if two of them are dead.
> Early to bed and early to rise,
>   Makes a man healthy, wealthy, and wise.

Governments and newspapers began issuing almanacs in the 1800s. They included recipes and first-aid advice for injuries and snake bite. Gradually, the weather predictions were abandoned except in the *Old Farmer's Almanac*. This almanac, founded in 1793, continues today with little reference value but an entertaining old-time flavor, still (some say accurately) predicting the weather and giving the rising and setting of the moon and sun.

Today's almanacs rarely preach and they deal with much more than just the calendar. Almanacs now have a great amount of facts and miscellaneous information in table form. Since they are published annually, much of the information is associated with a single year but modern almanacs have more and more historical information.

The major almanacs are the *Information Please Almanac, Atlas and Yearbook*, the *New York Times Encyclopedic Almanac*, the *Reader's Digest Almanac and Yearbook*, and the *World Almanac and Book of Facts*.

These give, to mention but a few items, chronologies of events of the previous year, facts about countries and their governments, lots of statistics on populations, elections, etc., and lists of colleges, of societies and associations, and of famous people.

Some of the special facts now appearing in almanacs are illustrated in this sampling. The reader can find:

> the distances between major cities,
> a list of famous waterfalls with location and height,
> a brief description of major art museum collections,
> postal information,
> the length of the Great Lakes,
> the state mottos (California's is "Eureka, I have found it.")
> pictures of the flags of the world.

With a frank admission of prejudice on the part of this guide, the *New York Times Encyclopedic Almanac* is recommended for its "encyclopedic" features such as a calendar of the events of 100 years ago, a list of endangered wildlife, a dictionary of medical symptons, and many full length articles by internationally respected authors.

There are also almanacs covering special subjects. For example, the *Negro Almanac* lists facts and figures pertaining to black history, and biographical information on black personalities.

Other countries also publish almanacs with their own emphasis. A well known one is Whitaker's *Almanack*, published in Great Britain.

Atlases, in many ways, are graphic illustrations of the facts found in almanacs. An atlas is a collection of maps and a map is a representation of the earth's surface or part of it (there are also maps of the sky). The map is an ancient form and has been found on a Babylonian clay tablet dating from as early as 2300 B.C. "Atlas" has come to mean a book of maps because the figure of Atlas (from Greek mythology) was used by the famous geographer Mercator on the title page of his map collections in the 16th century.

Today, maps are valuable not only because they describe places through lines indicating boundaries and roads but also because they can illustrate information such as the elevation of land, crops, rainfall, population and temperature through the use of symbols (dots, circles, triangles, etc.) and colors. Each map has a key which defines what the symbols and colors stand for.

Maps may give the general features of a place and also show that place in relation to the surrounding area or the world. An accurate map is drawn to "scale"—for example, a certain number of miles per inch. Then the reader can measure the distance on the map and figure the real distance on the earth's surface.

The introduction to *Goode's World Atlas* (listed below) has a good explanation of how to read maps and so does the *World Book Encyclopedia*. Most atlases and encyclopedias also explain the subject and if you use maps it is best to read some of this "get acquainted" material. The easiest way to locate something in an atlas is to check the index (an alphabetical list of cities and other features represented on the maps); this will give you the page or map number and two symbols—a letter and a number—that can be used to find what you want on the map.

One of the finest atlases is the *Times Atlas of the World*. The "Midcentury Edition" of this atlas is in five volumes (Vol. I: The World, Australia & East Asia. Vol. II: South-West Asia & Russia. Vol. III: Northern Europe. Vol IV: Southern Europe & Africa. Vol. V: The Americas) but there is also an excellent one volume "Comprehensive Edition." These beautiful atlases, published by the Times of London, are outstanding for their coverage, accuracy and handsome format. The Comprehensive Edition has a useful section on the resources of the world in relation to man's needs, a glossary of geographical terms, and a table of geographical comparisons so you can see at a glance that our Mt. McKinley is not as high as Asia's Everest but is higher than Tanzania's Kilimanjaro. Both editions of the *Times Atlas of the World* provide many inset maps of cities (Shanghai, Chicago, Brussels, New Orleans, etc.). The Comprehensive Edition combines the index-gazetteers of the Midcentury Edition in one alphabet and includes the English as well as the vernacular forms of place names (Florence as well as Firenze).

Gazetteers (geographical name dictionaries or indexes which usually include brief factual information about each place) are discussed in the Geography section of this guide. They are often used in tandem with atlases.

Goode's World Atlas is a student atlas, containing many world maps showing climate, rainfall, population, products, etc. It has maps of areas—polar regions, North America, South America, Europe, Asia and Africa—and also has the United States given in section maps, not state by state. Goode's has a "name pronouncing" index.

The *Rand McNally New Cosmopolitan World Atlas* has maps covering the physical and political world, the solar system, world history and American history. This atlas has individual maps of each American state.

Two other valuable world atlases are the *National Geographic Atlas of the World* and the *Hammond Medallion World Atlas*.

If you wanted to know the student population of Minot, North Dakota, the time difference between Alaska and Arabia, and the number of post offices in Boulder, Colorado, you'd find it in an atlas—the *Rand McNally Commercial Atlas and Marketing Guide*. Issued annually, this atlas has maps of general U.S. information and detailed commercial information in individual state maps. It includes transportation maps showing mileage and driving times, railroad and airline information, etc. Emphasis is on the U.S. but there are also sections on Canada and other parts of the world.

History can be represented in maps, too, and sometimes the reader can get a better understanding of certain alliances between countries or wars over boundaries by seeing them on a map. The term historical atlas is applied to one which is made up of maps illustrating past events or periods of history. It is not simply a collection of old maps. For example, the location and extent of the Navaho or Chickasaw Indian tribes in 1650 are shown in Paullin's *Atlas of the Historical Geography of the United States*. This atlas has many fascinating maps on explorations, elections, religious denominations, cities from 1775 to 1803, and the foreign born populations of the U.S.

Two historical atlases covering the world are *Muir's New School Atlas of Universal History* and Shepherd's *Historical Atlas*. Shepherd's covers the world from 1450 B.C. to modern times and has maps that are stuffed with information. A single map, for example, on the Westward Development of the U.S. shows all of the following and more:

Routes of the "Forty-Niners"
Santa Fe Trail
Route of Lewis and Clark
Forts and Trading Posts
Routes of the Pony Express
Principal land grants
Population centers
Agricultural centers.

There are historical atlases covering certain countries (Adams' *Atlas of American History*) or certain periods of time (Heyden's *Atlas of the Classical World*) and some atlases deal with certain subjects such as Bible or literary history. The history of war is examined in the *West Point Atlas of American Wars*, which includes maps of campaigns, battles, etc., from Colonial Wars to the Korean War. The list is endless.

So an atlas can be an excellent way to visualize the past and, of course, the use of a map is a better way to get from place to place than the Hansel and Gretel bread crumb method.

BIBLIOGRAPHY: ALMANACS AND ATLASES

ALMANACS

Information Please Almanac, Atlas and Yearbook. Ed. by Dan Golenpaul. New York, Simon & Schuster, 1947 to date. (Annual.)

Negro Almanac. Ed. By Harry A. Ploski and Roscoe C. Brown, Jr. Bellwether, 1967. (New edition due out in late 1970.)

New York Times Encyclopedic Almanac. New York, The New York Times Company, 1970 (Annual.)

Reader's Digest Almanac and Yearbook. Pleasantville, N.Y., Reader's Digest Association, 1966 to date. (Annual.)

Whitaker, Joseph. *Almanack.* London, J. Whitaker & Sons, 1869 to date. (Annual.)

World Almanac and Book of Facts. New York, Newspaper Enterprise Association, Inc., 1868 to date. (Annual.)

ATLASES

Adams, James Truslow. *Atlas of American History*. New York, Scribner, 1943.

Goode's World Atlas. 12th ed. Ed. by Edward B. Espenshade, Jr. Chicago, Rand McNally, 1964.

Hammond Medallion World Atlas. New Perspective Edition. Maplewood, N.J., C. S. Hammond & Co., 1966.

Heyden, A. A. M. van der and Scullard, Howard Hayes. *Atlas of the Classical World*. London, Nelson, 1959.

Muir's New School Atlas of Universal History. Ed. by R. F. Treharne and Harold Fullard. London, George Philip, 1960.

National Geographic Atlas of the World. Enlarged 2d edition. Melville Bell Grosvenor, Editor-in-chief. Washington, D.C., National Geographic Society, 1966.

Paullin, Charles Oscar. *Atlas of the Historical Geography of the United States*. Ed. by John K. Wright. Washington, New York, pub. jointly by the Carnegie Institute of Washington and the American Geographical Society, 1932.

Rand McNally Commercial Atlas and Marketing Guide. 101st ed. Chicago, Rand McNally, 1970. (Annual.)

Rand McNally New Cosmopolitan World Atlas. Chicago, Rand McNally, 1968.

Shepherd, William Robert. *Historical Atlas*. 9th ed. New York, Barnes and Noble, 1964.

Times Atlas of the World. Midcentury edition, ed. by John Bartholomew. London, Times Publishing Company, Ltd., 1955-1959. 5 vols.

Times Atlas of the World. Comprehensive edition; Boston, Houghton Mifflin, 1967.

U.S. Military Academy, West Point. Dept. of Military Art and Engineering. *The West Point Atlas of American Wars*. Chief ed., Vincent J. Esposito. New York, Praeger, 1959. 2 vols.

BIOGRAPHY

IT's BEEN suggested that biography should be written by an enemy. The implication is, of course, that truth would then have a better chance of emerging. But the cynic who made the claim probably was not acquainted with some of the excellent sources of biographical information not, ostensibly at least, written by enemies.

INFORMATION ABOUT PEOPLE PAST . . .

The *Dictionary of American Biography* is known for its scholarly articles and its objectivity. Note the following candid account of Andrew Johnson when he took the oath of office as Vice President at Lincoln's second inauguration:

> ". . . His health was impaired, and only Lincoln's urgent request hurried him to Washington in time for the inaugural ceremonies. The result was most unfortunate, for Johnson, when he took the oath of office, was under the influence of liquor . . . No doubt the faux pas was due to illness and exhaustion, but it gave malice something to feed upon."

The *DAB*, as this multivolume set is nicknamed, does not include the living. It covers only famous Americans of the past and it is exact about some legends, too. If you look up Molly Pitcher, for example, you will be referred to an interesting biography under her real name, Mary Ludwig Hays McCauley.

The *Dictionary of National Biography*, or the *DNB*, includes men and women in British history and this set was the model for the American series. It was edited by two scholars, one of whom, Leslie Stephen, was the father of author Virginia Woolf. In both of these sets the articles are signed and followed by bibliographies. Those are indications of reliable and thorough reference materials. Some early American colonists appear in both sets since they were first British and then American.

The articles in both the *DAB* and the *DNB* vary in length. Some run less than a page and some, dealing with important figures like George Washington, are several pages long.

Other works dealing with historical people but with only very brief articles are: *Who Was Who In America: Historical Volume, 1607-1896* and *Who Was Who in America* (four volumes covering the years from 1897-1968). (For a typical Who's Who entry see sample under Who's Who in America.)

Two one-volume dictionaries which have brief identifications of people both living and dead and of all nations are *Webster's Biographical Dictionary* and *Chambers's Biographical Dictionary*.

If you have a name you can't identify the best place to look first is the *New Century Cyclopedia of Names*. This three volume work includes persons, places, literary characters, works of art, plays and operas as well as real people. Mythological and legendary persons are listed. Under "Baker" the cyclopedia identifies by that name:

> a city,
> a mountain,
> a lake,
> an island,
> the battle of Baker,
> twenty-nine people,
> and one pseudonym.

Some living people are included in this naming of names.

INFORMATION ABOUT PEOPLE TODAY . . .

Current Biography has interesting articles about people in the news here and abroad. It is issued monthly and then as an annual cumulated volume. The biographies generally are one or two pages long. A perusal of a few recent years reveals the following variety of facts:

Bob Dylan was born Robert Zimmerman but officially changed his name in 1962 in honor of the poet Dylan Thomas, whom he admired.

As a child, Coretta King, widow of Dr. Martin Luther King, Jr., walked five miles each day to a one-room schoolhouse.

French ski champion Jean-Claude Killy started skiing at the age of three.

Cesar Chavez, Mexican-American organizer of migratory farm workers, grew up in a series of labor camps where home was a tar-paper shack, and he attended more than thirty elementary schools scattered along the family's itinerary.

Julia Child, the TV cook, majored in history while in college and wanted to be a spy during World War II. She didn't take up cooking until she was over thirty.

Popular Yiddish writer Isaac Bashevis Singer says of his early life: "I was born with the feeling that I am part of an unlikely adventure, something that couldn't have happened, but happened just the same. The atmosphere of adventure permeated my home . . ."

Dionne Warwick's professional name derives from a misspelling in one of her early recording contracts. She was born Marie Dionne Warrick and began her career as a gospel singer.

For brief biographical data about the living the books in the Who's Who series are useful. Some of these are: *Who's Who* (British and a few other people of international reputation),

Who's Who In America, and *Who's Who in (various countries).* The Europa *International Who's Who* covers a wide range from Jean Paul Getty to Mao Tse-tung. Here is a sample from *Who's Who in America* of the typical, brief Who's Who entry:

VONNEGUT, Kurt, Jr., writer; b. Indpls., Nov. 11, 1922; s. Kurt and Edith (Lieber) V.; student Cornell U., 1940-42, U. Chgo., 1945-47; m. Jane Marie Cox, Sept. 1, 1945; children—Mark, Edith, Nanette, adopted nephews—James, Steven and Kurt Adams. Mng. editor Cornell Sun, 1942; reporter Chgo. City News Bur., 1946; pub. relations with Gen. Electric Co., 1947-50; free-lance writer, 1950-65; tchr. Hopefield Sch., Sandwich, Mass., 1965—; lectr. Writers Workshop, U. Ia., 1965-67. Served with Inf. AUS, 1942-45. Decorated Purple Heart; Guggenheim Fellow 1967-68. Unitarian. Author: (novels) Player Piano, 1951, Sirens of Titan, 1959, Mother Night, 1961, Cat's Cradle, 1963, God Bless You, Mr. Rosewater, 1964; (story collection) Welcome To The Mon ey House, 1968; (novel) Slaughterhouse-Five, 1969; also short stories, articles, revs. Address: Scudder's Lane, West Barnstable, Mass. 02668.

INFORMATION ABOUT PEOPLE IN SPECIAL FIELDS . . .

There are biographical dictionaries in almost all fields but some on authors, scientists, and scholars are of particular interest and are good examples of specialized biographies.

Twentieth Century Authors (1942) and its First Supplement (1955), edited by Kunitz, Haycraft and Colby, are outstanding sources. The articles contain lists of works by and about the authors and the sketches are very readable. Here is J. D. Salinger quoted:

> "I'm aware that a number of my friends will be saddened, or shocked, or shocked-saddened, over some of my chapters of *The Catcher in the Rye.* Some of my best friends are children. In fact, all of my best friends are children. It's almost unbearable to me to realize that my book will be kept on a shelf out of their reach."

Kunitz and Haycraft have done other books on authors: *American Authors 1600-1900, British Authors Before 1800, British Authors of the Nineteenth Century,* and *Junior Book of Authors.* Another book about authors of books for young people is *More Junior Authors,* edited by Muriel Fuller.

Contemporary Authors: A Bio-bibliographical Guide to Current Authors and Their Work is an up-to-date source and includes many little-known authors. Each brief article is followed by a list of all the author's published works.

Another work dealing with authors is the *Cyclopedia of World Authors,* which covers the authors whose works are included in *Masterpieces of World Literature in Digest Form* (see Books and Literature). The entry gives biographical details, critical evaluations, and a list of each writer's principal works.

Two other highly regarded works are the eight volume *American Men of Science* (with biographies in the physical and biological sciences and in the social and behavioral sciences) and the *Directory of American Scholars,* a four volume set (with biographies of U.S. and Canadian scholars in English, Speech, Drama, Foreign Languages, Linguistics, Philology, Philosophy, Religion and Law).

INDEXES TO BIOGRAPHY . . .

Biography Index is a quarterly, cumulative index to biographical material in both books and magazines. Each issue contains a useful index by professions and occupations.

The *New York Times Index* (described in more detail in the Chapter on "Magazines and Newspapers") is the key to biographical sketches and news stories that have appeared in that newspaper. These have the advantage of showing the man or woman "in context." That is, the subject is seen in relation to his time, to the news of that day and that year in the U.S. and in the world.

BIBLIOGRAPHY: BIOGRAPHY

American Authors 1600-1900. Ed. by S. J. Kunitz and H. Haycraft. New York, Wilson, 1938.

American Men of Science. Ed. by the Jaques Cattell Press, 11th ed. New York, Bowker, 1965-1968. 8 vols.

Biography Index: A Cumulative Index to Biographical Material in Books and Magazines. New York, Wilson, Sept. 1946 to date.

British Authors Before 1800. Ed. by S. J. Kunitz and H. Haycraft. New York, Wilson, 1952.

British Authors of the Nineteenth Century. Ed. by S. J. Kunitz and H. Haycraft. New York, Wilson, 1936.

Chambers's Biographical Dictionary. Ed. by J. O. Thorne. New York, St. Martin's, 1962.

Contemporary Authors: A Bio-bibliographical Guide to Current Authors and Their Work. Ed. by James N. Ethridge. Detroit, Gale Research, 1962 to date. (Semiannual.)

Current Biography. New York, Wilson, 1940 to date.

Cyclopedia of World Authors. Ed. by Frank N. Magill. New York, Harper, 1958.

Dictionary of American Biography. New York, Scribner, 1928-1958. 20 vols., index and Supplements One and Two.

Dictionary of National Biography. Ed. by Leslie Stephen and Sidney Lee. London, Oxford University Press, 1922. 22 vols. 6 supplements.

Directory of American Scholars. Ed. by the Jaques Cattell Press, 5th ed. New York, Bowker, 4 vols.

International Who's Who. London, Europa, 1935 to date.

Junior Book of Authors. Ed. by S. J. Kunitz and H. Haycraft. 2nd ed. rev. New York, Wilson, 1951.

More Junior Authors. Ed. by Muriel Fuller. New York, Wilson, 1963.

New Century Cyclopedia of Names. Ed. by C. L. Barnhart. New York, Appleton-Century-Crofts, 1954. 3 vols.

New York Times Index. New York, New York Times, 1913 to date.

Twentieth Century Authors. Ed. by S. J. Kunitz and H. Haycraft. First Supplement by S. J. Kunitz and V. Colby. New York, Wilson, 1942, 1955.

Webster's Biographical Dictionary. 1st ed., reprinted Springfield, Merriam, 1969.

Who's Who. London, Black, 1849 to date. (Annual.)

Who's Who In America. Chicago, Marquis, 1899 to date. (Biennial.)

Who Was Who In America. Chicago, Marquis, 1942-1968. 4 vols.

Who Was Who In America: Historical Volume, 1607-1896. A component volume of Who's Who in American History. Chicago, Marquis, 1963.

DICTIONARIES

W<small>HAT</small>'s the difference between abjure and adjure, or anecdote and antidote, or even ant and aunt? How about allusion, elusion, illusion and delusion? What do the initials LSD really stand for and how do you pronounce faux pas?

If you can get through life without using a dictionary then you're practicing thaumaturgy.

Dictionaries have been around for a long time and they're getting better all the time. The first English dictionary was compiled in 1604 by a schoolmaster, Robert Cawdrey, and it carried the straightforward title *A Table Alphabeticall Conteyning and Teaching the True Writing and Understanding of Hard Usuall English Wordes*. Cawdrey had so little faith in the intelligence of the reader that he instructs in the preface: "If thou be desirous (gentle reader) rightly and readily to understand and profit by this Table, and such like, then thou must learn the alphabet . . ."

Certainly it helps to know the alphabet because a dictionary, of course, is an alphabetical arrangement of words with their meaning, derivation and pronunciation.

Two famous works in the history of the dictionary are Samuel Johnson's *A Dictionary of the English Language*, which appeared in 1755, and Noah Webster's *American Dictionary of the English Language*, which first appeared in 1828.

Cawdrey's dictionary contained about 3,000 words. Today's unabridged dictionaries contain hundreds of thousands of words. An "unabridged" dictionary is very large and has the most complete list of words. An "abridged" dictionary is a smaller version with fewer words and shorter definitions but retains the features of the unabridged work. Strictly speaking, a "desk dictionary" is still smaller, being a general purpose work with only a selection of the words of a language. However, the phrase "desk dictionary" is sometimes loosely used to apply to any abridged dictionary.

UNABRIDGED DICTIONARIES

The main unabridged dictionaries are:

Funk & Wagnalls New Standard Dictionary (1963) contains about 450,000 words including 65,000 proper names. It gives current meanings first, provides pronunciation, etymology (the history of a word) and geographical entries. The appendix has a list of foreign words and phrases, rules for simplified spelling, and disputed pronunciations. (It also has a list of places but the population figures given are now out of date.)

Random House Dictionary of the English Language (1966) has about 260,000 words and emphasizes words and phrases recently in use in the language. It also carries personal and place names, and encyclopedic information such as a list of colleges, an atlas, a list of reference books, etc. The most common meaning of a word is given first.

Webster's Third New International Dictionary (1961) contains about 450,000 words and does *not* include personal and place names. Current meaning is given last and, except for some abbreviations and symbols, the main entries are set in lower-case and capitalization is indicated within the definition in italics as "cap", "usu cap", "often cap", or "sometimes cap." This work was considered unconventional and "permissive" when it first appeared because it presents the language as it is now *used* and therefore includes many words regarded as colloquial and even incorrect. Regardless of the varying opinions, it is an extremely complete and careful work.

Unabridged dictionaries all define words and give examples of usage (and changes in meaning) in sentences and quotations. A note on the parts of speech gives the word's grammatical use (n. for noun, adv. for adverb, etc.). Popular phrases that include the key word are also given and defined (under "limb" the phrase "out on a limb" is defined). Derivations or the origins of words are indicated by giving the language a word comes from and its meaning in that language. > is the symbol that means "comes from."

The pronunciation key is given on each page in *Funk & Wagnalls* and *Random House*. The front of the book carries the key in *Webster's Third*.

There are full page illustrations in the unabridged dictionaries (showing birds, flowers, flags of the world, etc.) as well as small illustrations which accompany and clarify definitions.

Random House

A, First position; B, Second position; C, Third position; D, Fourth position; E, Fifth position

first′ posi′tion, *Ballet.* a position of the feet in which the heels are back to back and the toes point out to the sides.

Webster's Third

By permission. From Webster's Third New International Dictionary © 1966 by G. & C. Merriam Co., Publishers of the Merriam-Webster Dictionaries.

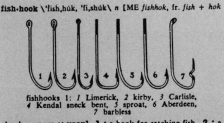

fish-hook \ 'fish,hùk, 'fi,shùk *n* [ME *fishhok,* fr. *fish* + *hok*]

fishhooks 1: *1* Limerick, *2* kirby, *3* Carlisle, *4* Kendal sneck bent, *5* sproat, *6* Aberdeen, *7* barbless

hook — more at HOOK] **1 :** a hook for catching fish **2 :** a large hook with a pendant to the end of which the fish tackle is hooked in fishing an anchor

gui-tar′, 1 gi-tär′; 2 ĝi-tär′, *n.* A musical instrument with a body and neck somewhat like a violin, and usually six strings, three of gut and three of silk spun over with silver wire, played by the fingers of one hand, while the notes are stopped by the fingers of the other on the frets of the neck. It is tuned as shown below, according to its written notation, but sounds an octave lower. [< F. *gui-ture,* < L. *cithara,* < Gr. *kithara,* kind of lyre.]
Manner of Tuning Guitar. — **gui-tar′ fid″dle,** *n.*
Mus. A five-stringed viol, predecessor of the violin, flat-bodied like the guitar.—

Funk & Wagnalls

An example of the comprehensiveness of the unabridged dictionaries is seen in the treatment of the word "the" in *Webster's Third*. It's given almost two columns.

ABRIDGED AND DESK TYPE DICTIONARIES

The *American Heritage Dictionary of the English Language* is an excellent new (1969) work. It is new enough, for example, to indicate under "grass" that a secondary use of the word is slang for marijuana. This dictionary is very up-to-date and based on a high standard of good English.

Webster's Seventh New Collegiate Dictionary is a very good, all purpose dictionary for students and general readers. First published in 1963, it is continuously revised so each new printing contains minor changes and corrections.

Funk & Wagnalls Standard College Dictionary is based on the comprehensive Funk & Wagnalls Standard Dictionary-International Edition and contains practical guides to punctuation, capitalization, signs and symbols, etc. First published in 1963, it is reprinted annually with revisions and corrections.

Thorndike-Barnhart Comprehensive Desk Dictionary is one of the best and most popular smaller dictionaries though it is not as comprehensive as those listed above. This work presents up-to-date information on a basic vocabulary and has many examples of proper usage.

For a feeling of how dictionaries vary, here is an example showing how the same word (peace) is treated in the unabridged *Webster's Third* and in the abridged *American Heritage Dictionary of the English Language*.

Webster's Third has more details, more illustrations showing an appropriate use of the word in context (the matter in angle

WEBSTER'S THIRD NEW INTERNATIONAL DICTIONARY *Unabridged**

¹peace \'pēs\ *n* -s *often attrib* [ME *pes, pees, pais,* fr. OF *pes, pais,* fr. L *pac-, pax peace;* akin to L *pacisci* to agree, contract — more at PACT] **1 a :** freedom from civil clamor and confusion **:** a state of public quiet (~ and order were finally restored in the town) **b :** a state of security or order within a community provided for by law, custom, or public opinion — often used with *the* (a breach of the ~) **2 :** a mental or spiritual condition marked by freedom from disquieting or oppressive thoughts or emotions **:** calmness of mind and heart **:** serenity of spirit (the bitter, restless struggling of the last months gave way to ~ —Rose Macaulay) (I have been in perfect ~ and contentment; I never have had one doubt —J.H. Newman) (a ~ of mind because you could no longer be surprised —Theodore Cloete) (farewell and ~ be with you) — compare PEACE OF GOD **3 a :** a tranquil state of freedom from outside disturbance and harassment (decided to accept a year-round post . . . and have ~ to write —*Newsweek*) (now remembered sharply the ~ and quiet of the place —Sherwood Anderson) **b :** eternal repose (may he rest in ~) **4 :** harmony in human or personal relations **:** mutual concord and esteem (he knew that there would never be ~ again while they lived —Graham Greene) **5 a** (1) **:** a state of mutual concord between governments **:** absence of hostilities or war (he had given the world ~, and the world now turned to him for security —John Buchan) (2) **:** the period of such freedom from war (a ~ of 50 years) **b :** a pact or agreement to end hostilities or to come together in amity between those who have been at war or in a state of enmity or dissension **:** a formal reconciliation between contending parties, *esp* **:** a peace treaty (signed ~ in the spring of 1918 —C.E. Black & E.C. Helmreich) (offered the possibility of a negotiated ~ —*N.Y. Times*) **6 :** absence of activity and noise **:** deep stillness **:** QUIETNESS (the ~ of the woods) (the ~ of sky and mountain) **7 :** one that makes, gives, or maintains tranquillity (God is our only ~) — **at peace** *adv* **:** in a state of concord or tranquillity (a world once more *at peace*) (the problem was settled and his mind was *at peace*) (help man live *at peace* with his unconscious — *Time*)
²peace \'\ *vi* -ED -ING -S [ME *peesen,* fr. *pes, pees, pais* peace (n.)] **:** to become quiet or still **:** be, become, or keep silent (when the thunder would not ~ at my bidding —Shak.) — often used interjectionally
peace-abil-i-ty \͵pēsə'biləd-ē, -lətē, -i\ *n* **:** PEACEABLENESS (snore himself to ~ —P.A. Rollins)
peace-able \'pēsabəl\ *adj* [ME *pesible, pesable, paisible,* fr. MF *pesible, paisible,* fr. *pes, pais* peace + *-ible* — more at PEACE] **1 a :** disposed to peace **:** having an amicable disposition disinclined to strife **:** not contentious or quarrelsome (the quiet, humble, modest and ~ person —William Cowper) (his tongue was not always ~ —W.R.Inge) **b :** lacking noisiness or restlessness **:** quietly behaved **:** CALM (was pleased to see how ~ the horse had become) **2 :** marked by freedom from war, strife, hostilities, or disorder (in the most ~ and orderly manner, without the smallest sign of tumult or sedition in the city — J.G.Frazer) (the company . . . in times makes chiefly freight cars —E.D.Kennedy) **syn** see PACIFIC
peace-able-ness *n* -ES [ME *pesiblenesse,* fr. *pesible, pesable, paisible* peaceable + *-nesse* -ness] **:** the quality or state of being peaceable
peace-ably \-blē -bli\ *adv* [ME *pesibly, paisibly,* fr. *pesible, paisible* + -y] **1 :** in a peaceable and friendly manner **:** without contention or strife (possible for more than one state to survive comparatively ~ in the same state —Alfred Cobban) **2 :** without subjection to annoyance or confusion **:** in peace **:** QUIETLY (disturb him not; let him pass ~ —Shak.)
peace belt *n* **:** a wampum belt used to symbolize peace among No American Indians

peacebreaker \'͵ˌˌ\ *n* **:** a violator of peace or of the peace **:** a perpetrator of strife
peacebreaking \'͵ˌˌ\ *n* **:** the action of violating peace **:** the commission of a breach of the peace
peace democrat *n, usu cap P&D* **:** a Democrat in the northern states advocating peaceful measures as opposed to prosecution of the Civil War
peace dollar *n* **:** a silver dollar of the U.S. struck from 1921 to 1928 and in 1934 and 1935 to commemorate the peace at the end of World War I
peace-ful \'pēsfəl\ *adj, sometimes* **peacefuller;** *sometimes* **peacefullest** [ME *paisful, pesful,* fr. *pais, pes, pees* peace + *-ful* — more at PEACE] **1 :** PEACEABLE 1 (the ~ comportment of the seals had quieted my alarm —Jack London) (the modest man becomes bold . . . or the impetuous prudent and ~ —W.M.Thackeray) **2 :** marked by, conducive to, or enjoying peace, quiet, or calm **:** untroubled by conflict, agitation, or commotion (the feeling . . . that we as neighbors could settle any disputes in ~ fashion —F.D.Roosevelt) (rocky promontories shelter ~ bays —Samuel Van Valkenburg & Ellsworth Huntington) **3 :** of or relating to a state or time of peace (a bomb material as well as a ~ fuel —Oliver Townsend) **4 :** devoid of violence or force **:** without recourse to warlike methods (all the political groups . . . employed ~ tactics —*Collier's Yr Bk.*) (~ procedures . . . mediation, investigation and conciliation —*Current History*) **syn** see CALM, PACIFIC
peace-ful-ly \-fəlē, -li\ *adv* **:** in a peaceful manner (cattle which ~ browse —Tom Marvel) (a ~ inclined and responsible government —Vera M. Dean)
peace-ful-ness \-fəlnəs\ *n* -ES **:** the quality or state of being peaceful **:** the neighborliness of the parish is proverbial (*Inner Guide Series La.*)
peace-keeper \'͵ˌˌ\ *n* **:** a maintainer of peace or of the peace **:** a pacific country or person
peace-less \'pēsləs\ *adj* **:** having no peace — **peace-less-ness** *n* -ES
peacemaker \'͵ˌˌ\ *n* [ME *peace maker,* fr. *pease, pes, pees, pais* peace + *maker*] **:** one that makes or seeks to make peace esp. by reconciling parties or persons at variance
¹**peacemaking** \'͵ˌˌ\ *n* **:** the action of bringing about peace
²**peacemaking** \'\ *adj* **:** bringing about peace or done in an effort to bring about peace
peacemonger \'͵ˌˌ\ *n* **:** PEACEMAKER; *esp* **:** one making or seeking peace unrealistically or at the expense of honor — usu. used disparagingly
peacemongering \'͵ˌ(ˌ)ˌ\ *adj* **:** PEACEMAKING — usu. used disparagingly
peace offensive *n* **:** a campaign designed to serve the interests of a nation by the expression of wishes to end a war or of intentions to resolve conflicts peacefully and thus cause hostile or unfriendly nations to relax their efforts or become less vigilant
peace offering *n* **1 :** an ancient Hebrew votive, freewill, or thank offering **2 :** a gift or service to procure peace or reconciliation
peace officer *n* **:** a civil officer (as a sheriff, constable, policeman) whose duty it is to preserve the public peace
peace of god *n cap G* **:** the peace of heart which is the gift of God **2** *usu cap P & cap G* **:** an exemption from attack in feudal warfare urged by the church beginning in the latter part of the 9th century for all consecrated persons and places and later for all who claimed the protection of the church (as pilgrims, the poor) — compare TRUCE OF GOD
peace pipe *n* **:** CALUMET
peaces *pl of* PEACE, *pres 3d sing of* PEACE
peacetime \'͵ˌˌ\ *n* **:** a time when a nation is not at war (as anxious to save lives in ~ as . . . in wartime — *Tomorrow*)

*By permission. From Webster's Third New International Dictionary © 1966 by G. & C. Merriam Co., Publishers of the Merriam-Webster Dictionaries.

AMERICAN HERITAGE DICTIONARY OF THE ENGLISH LANGUAGE *Abridged*

peace (pēs) *n.* **1.** The absence of war or other hostilities. **2.** An agreement or treaty to end hostilities: *the Peace of Westphalia.* **3.** Freedom from quarrels and disagreement; harmonious relations: *They made peace with each other.* **4.** Public security; law and order: *disturbing the peace.* **5.** Inner contentment; calm; serenity: *peace of mind.* —**at peace. 1.** In a state of tranquillity; serene. **2.** Free from strife. —**hold** (or **keep**) **one's peace.** To be silent. —**keep the peace.** To maintain or observe law and order. [Middle English *pes, pais,* from Old French, from Latin *pāx* (stem *pāc-*). See **pag-** in Appendix.*]
peace·a·ble (pē'sə-bəl) *adj.* **1.** Inclined or disposed to peace; promoting calm: *They met in a peaceable spirit.* **2.** Peaceful; undisturbed. —**peace'a·ble·ness** *n.* —**peace'a·bly** *adv.*
Peace Corps. A Federal government organization, set up in 1961, that trains and sends American volunteers abroad to work with people of developing countries on projects for technological, agricultural, and educational improvement.
peace·ful (pēs'fəl) *adj.* **1.** Undisturbed by strife, turmoil, or disagreement; tranquil. **2.** Opposed to strife; peaceable. **3.** Of

or characteristic of a condition of peace. —See Synonyms at calm. —**peace'ful·ly** *adv.* —**peace'ful·ness** *n.*
peace·mak·er (pēs'mā'kər) *n.* **1.** One who makes peace, especially by settling the disputes of others. **2.** A revolver, especially the 1873 Colt model, used by law officers on the U.S. frontier. —**peace'mak'ing** *n. & adj.*
peace offering. 1. Any offering made to an adversary in the interests of peace or reconciliation. **2.** An offering made to God in thanksgiving, especially a sacrificial offering as prescribed by Levitical law. Leviticus 3:2–6.
peace officer. A law officer, such as a sheriff, responsible for maintaining civil peace.
peace pipe. The calumet (*see*).
Peace River. A river rising in east-central British Columbia, Canada, and flowing 1,065 miles east and northeast to join the Slave River in northeastern Alberta.
peace·time (pēs'tīm') *n.* A time of absence of war. —**peace'-time'** *adj.*

brackets ‹ › with the slung dash ⌐ standing for the word "peace"),
many more words between "peace" and "peach," and no capitalization except for an indication of it within the definition of
"peace of god." The *American Heritage Dictionary* shows
proper names and geographical entries so it has "Peace Corps"
and "Peace River," which are not given in Webster's since the
latter does not include names. The American Heritage also
shows capitalization in the names.

For complete, detailed information on the many dictionaries
that are available see *Home Reference Books in Print; A Comparative Analysis.* This is especially useful if you are going to
purchase a dictionary.

THE OXFORD ENGLISH DICTIONARY

This thirteen volume dictionary must be singled out for special attention. It is the most authoritative dictionary of the English language and its purpose is to give the etymology or history of all the words in the language from the year 1150 to
its publication (1888-1933). It shows how each word came into
the language and the changes in spelling and meaning that
have occurred. Quotations from the first known use of the word
to the latest are given. Some of the words in it have a very
different meaning today:

> **Hippy,** *a. colloq.* [f. HIP *sb.*3] = HIPPISH.
> **1891** *Temple Bar Mag.* Aug. 478 [She] led him such an
> awful life, No wonder he was hippy.

and Hippish is defined as "somewhat hypochondriacal;
low-spirited."

Here's another:

> **Groovy** (grū'vi), *a.* [f. GROOVE *sb.* + -Y 1.]
> **1.** Of or pertaining to a groove; resembling
> a groove.
> **1853** O. BYRNE *Artisan's Hand-bk.* 383 Its main purpose
> is to keep the surface of the ivory slightly lubricated, so
> that the rag may not hang to it and wear it into rings or
> groovy marks.
> **2.** *fig.* Having a tendency to run in 'grooves'
> (cf. GROOVE *sb.* 4). *colloq.*
> **1882** *Railway News* 12 Aug. 245/1 Railway managers are
> apt..to get a little 'groovy'. **1893** FARMER *Slang,* Groovy,
> settled in habit; limited in mind. **1896** *Blackw. Mag.*
> July 96 Schoolmasters as a class are extremely groovy.

Schoolmasters today would probably be pleased to be thought of as groovy. These are rather short samples; many entries are longer. The OED goes on for four pages with the unhappy word "war."

There is often confusion over its title. It was first published as the *New English Dictionary on Historical Principles*, then later reissued as the *Oxford English Dictionary* and both of these are often abbreviated, the first as the *NED*, the second as the *OED*. And there's still another. It is also called Murray's Dictionary because the main editor was Sir James Augustus Henry Murray. Whatever the name used, call it interesting.

There is an abridged edition of the OED, the *Shorter Oxford English Dictionary on Historical Principles*, in two volumes, which also serves as a supplement to the OED because it has additional words.

SPECIAL DICTIONARIES
AND LANGUAGE HANDBOOKS

There is no such thing as a last word on the subject of grammar and usage, but Fowler's *Dictionary of Modern English Usage* is thought to come closest to it. It is not always easy to use, however, since some of the headings of this British work are not familiar to an American student. But the 2nd edition (revised by Sir Ernest Gowers in 1965) has a classified guide in the front which helps the reader find the item he needs. This is an alphabetical arrangement of explanations of such things as fused participles, verbless sentences, and the proper use of such words as forwards or forward.

Two American books on the subject of usage are especially lucid and witty. *The Careful Writer* by Theodore M. Bernstein deals with split infinitives, punctuation, got vs. gotten, and though he doesn't completely condemn clichés he cautions against "curdled clichés." (It's in the lap of the cards. That hits

it right on the nutshell. He needs some money to tidy him over.
I was smoking like a chain.) Here is Bernstein's example of a
grammatical exception:

> **FLIED**
> You won't find it in most dictionaries, but *flied* is the past
> tense of *fly* in one specialized field: baseball. You could not say
> of the batter who hoisted a can of corn to the center fielder that
> he "flew out"; you must say he *flied out*.

A *Dictionary of Contemporary American Usage* by Bergen
and Cornelia Evans is a scholarly and informal book on modern
usage. It covers the basics and includes witty dividends like:

> **kith and kin** is a cliché, one of those meaningless
> phrases kept current by alliteration. A fitting
> punishment for anyone who uses it would be to
> require him to use the word *kith* at once in
> some other context. The chances are overwhelm-
> ing that he couldn't do it. The word meant
> originally those who are known to us, friends,
> fellow-countrymen, neighbors, acquaintances.
> It is related to the old word *couth*, known. In
> the stable societies of older times all of one's
> kin were probably kith, though not all who
> were kith were kin. When Middleton wrote, in
> 1620, *A maid that's neither kith nor kin to me*,
> he seems to have the proper distinction in mind.
> But for well over a century the two words have
> been assumed to be synonymous. Burns wrote
> *My lady's white, my lady's red,/ And kith and
> kin o' Cassillis' blude,* though one cannot be
> kith of blood.

Two important books tell you about related words and help
you find another word for one you may have already repeated
too many times. *Webster's Dictionary of Synonyms* gives words
with like meanings and includes antonyms, words with opposite
meanings. *Roget's International Thesaurus* groups snyonyms
and antonyms according to the ideas to which they relate.
There are various editions of Roget's Thesaurus; some require
use of the "pinpoint" index and one is alphabetized.

SLANG DICTIONARIES

Mathew's *A Dictionary of Americanisms* and Craigie's *Dictionary of American English on Historical Principles* give you, without a trace of a smile, very serious discussions of words like hot dog, hamburger and meathead. Wentworth and Flexner's *Dictionary of American Slang* includes rhyming terms, Black Slang, Pig Latin, and lists of suffixes like—nik (beatnik, folknik, neatnik) and prefix words like soul—(soul brother, soul food, soul music), etc.

Another standard work on slang is Eric Partridge's *Dictionary of Slang and Unconventional English*, which uses the historical approach.

There's a "dictionary of" just about every subject and many are included in this guide under specific subject headings. There are rhyming dictionaries, abbreviation dictionaries and many on music, literature and sports. There is plenty of printed proof that there will never be a last word on any subject.

BIBLIOGRAPHY: DICTIONARIES

American Heritage Dictionary of the English Language. William Morris, ed. Boston, American Heritage and Houghton Mifflin, 1969.

Bernstein, Theodore M. *The Careful Writer.* New York, Atheneum, 1965.

Craigie, Sir William, and James R. Hulbert. *A Dictionary of American English on Historical Principles.* Chicago, University of Chicago Press, 1936-1944. 4 vols.

Evans, Bergen and Cornelia. *A Dictionary of Contemporary American Usage.* New York, Random House, 1957.

Fowler, Henry Watson. *Dictionary of Modern English Usage.* 2d ed., rev. by Sir Ernest Gowers. Oxford, Clarendon Press, 1965.

Funk & Wagnalls New Standard Dictionary of the English Language. New York, Funk & Wagnalls, 1963.

Funk & Wagnalls Standard College Dictionary. New York, Funk & Wagnalls, 1968.

Home Reference Books in Print. S. Padraig Walsh, comp. New York, Bowker, 1969.

Mathews, Mitford M. *A Dictionary of Americanisms on Historical Principles.* Chicago, University of Chicago Press, 1951. 2 vols.

Murray, Sir James A. H. *New English Dictionary on Historical Principles.* Oxford, Clarendon Press, 1888-1933. 10 vols. and supplement. Reissued 1933 in 13 vols. under the title *Oxford English Dictionary. Shorter Oxford English Dictionary on Historical Principles.* Prepared by William Little, H. W. Fowler, J. Coulson. Rev. and ed. by C. T. Onions, 3d ed. with addenda. Oxford, Clarendon Press, 1962. 2 vols.

Partridge, Eric. *Dictionary of Slang and Unconventional English.* 6th ed. rev. and enl. New York, Macmillan, 1967.

Random House Dictionary of the English Language. Ed. by J. M. Stein. New York, Random House, 1966.

Roget's International Thesaurus. 3d ed. New York, Crowell, 1962.

Thorndike-Barnhart Comprehensive Desk Dictionary. Ed. by Clarence L. Barnhart. New York, Doubleday, 1967.

Webster's New Dictionary of Synonyms. Springfield, Mass., Merriam, 1968.

Webster's Seventh New Collegiate Dictionary. Springfield, Mass., Merriam, 1969.

Webster's Third New International Dictionary. Ed. by Philip Babcock Gove. Springfield, Mass., Merriam, 1961.

Wentworth, Harold, and Flexner, Stuart Berg. *Dictionary of American Slang.* Supplemented ed. New York, Crowell, 1967.

ENCYCLOPEDIAS

ENCYCLOPEDIA is a word of Greek origin which means the "circle of knowledge" of the ancients. It is indeed an ancient form of reference book.

Aristotle did something like an encyclopedia and the oldest is said to have been one dating from A.D. 77 by Pliny the Elder, a friendly but unlikely name which sounds like it belongs to a rock group.

So man has apparently always been eager to put together all he knows, in some kind of order, of course. That's what an encyclopedia is: "all" knowledge usually arranged alphabetically or by subject.

In recent years, a certain disdain for encyclopedias has become fashionable, probably because they are so easy to use (when did the difficult become equated with the best?) and because a teacher's requirement that students use other materials in addition to encyclopedias is misinterpreted as meaning to avoid altogether the use of encyclopedias.

In fact, encyclopedias are the best place to start to search a subject. An important beginning can be made in understanding a topic by reading the systematic summary in an encyclopedia. For here you can get the basic background information on a subject, the overview by an expert.

The *Americana*, the *Britannica*, and *Collier's* are all "adult" encyclopedias. The *World Book* ranges from "young people's" to "general adult" encyclopedia and *Compton's* is a "school" or "young people's" set. But don't quite believe those labels and what they imply. In some ways and on some subjects the *World Book* is of better service to an adult and the *Britannica* might be of more use to a young student.

Encyclopedias are usually kept up-to-date by annual year books which have the latest information on various subjects and personalities. Also, the major encyclopedias (all of those mentioned above) are produced through a program of "continuous revision." That means that editors are always revising and adding material and each year's issue of the set contains articles changed or added.

Collier's Encyclopedia, first published in 1949, has a popular though still comprehensive approach and is geared to modern interests. The index volume has a valuable study guide to many subjects and contains an excellent bibliography. Its style is popular and readable and its appearance is attractive.

Compton's Encyclopedia and Fact Index is geared to meet the requirements of the school curricula and so is aimed at children and young people. It is easy to use and comprehend and is still abundantly illustrated though the "pictured encyclopedia" has been dropped from the title. There is a fact-index at the end of each volume so the reader can quickly locate a single fact and find the information gathered from all volumes relating to the subject.

Encyclopaedia Britannica has a long and noble history. It was first printed in Scotland in 1771 by a "Society of Gentlemen," and has been American-owned and published since 1902. It is a fine work with detailed and scholarly—and sometimes ponderous—treatment of subjects. It is especially strong in art, history, politics and the biological sciences. It is probably the most comprehensive of all encyclopedias but use of the index is essential in locating smaller topics within a subject. The index volume also contains an atlas.

The Encyclopedia Americana first appeared in 1829. It has a reputation for being especially strong in science and technology probably because it was edited at one time by Frederick Converse Beach, who was also an editor of *Scientific American* magazine. It is of particular use for summaries of famous books, biography and for histories of the centuries. Treatment is scholarly and this encyclopedia carries short articles on small subjects as well as long, detailed articles.

The World Book Encyclopedia has a distinct, colorful personality. The format is perfect for quickly finding a fact or understanding the main points of a subject because the highlights of articles are brought forward in illustrations, chronological lists of important events, lists of people associated with the subject, etc. There is no index but a reading and study guide which organizes the contents into major divisions serves in place of an index and there are many cross references. This work combines the best of a young people's encyclopedia with the accuracy and overall plan of an adult encyclopedia.

ONE VOLUME ENCYCLOPEDIAS

The Columbia Encyclopedia is the best one volume encyclopedia but the present (3rd) edition was published in 1963 with only one 16 page supplement to update it in 1967. It contains short, concise, accurate articles on an astonishing number of subjects.

The Lincoln Library of Essential Information is a good, compact introduction to general knowledge. It is arranged in twelve subject areas but also contains an index and is useful for self-education.

SPECIAL SUBJECT ENCYCLOPEDIAS

There are many outstanding encyclopedias for special topics. Some of these will be discussed under the proper subject areas later in this guide. Two subject encyclopedias are mentioned here as examples. The *International Encyclopedia of the Social Sciences* has topical articles addressed to concepts, theories and methods in fields such as anthropology, history, political science and sociology. In this work, for example, there is a discussion of the concept of the "just war," of evolution, and an article on Sigmund Freud.

Another subject encyclopedia, the *Encyclopedia of Associations,* lists American organizations in all fields including business, government, science, medicine, education, religion, sports, etc. The entry for each association gives the name of the executive director, the founding date, address and purpose. A look at this book usually surprises readers because of the variety and number of groups. Have you heard of the National Cheerleaders Association? Maybe. But have you heard of these two: the International Wizard of Oz Club and the Society of the Whiskey Rebellion of 1794?

ABOUT ENCYCLOPEDIAS

If you're interested in some encyclopedic information about encyclopedias and especially if you are going to buy one, take a look at *General Encyclopedias in Print; A Comparative Analysis.*

The best way to get the feeling of the different personalities of encyclopedias is to pick any subject you're familiar with and see how it is treated in each work. Even a quick glance will tell you a lot. You'll find a tremendous amount of information packed into a small space and that's why an encyclopedia has been called an "intellectual bazaar."

BIBLIOGRAPHY: ENCYCLOPEDIAS

Collier's Encyclopedia. New York, Crowell-Collier Educational Corporation, 1970. 24 vols.

Columbia Encyclopedia. 3d ed. Edited by William Bridgewater and Seymour Kurtz. New York, Columbia University Press, 1963.

Compton's Encyclopedia and Fact Index. Chicago, F. E. Compton Company, 1970. 24 vols.

Encyclopedia Americana. New York, Americana Corporation, 1970. 30 vols.

Encyclopaedia Britannica. Chicago, Encyclopedia Britannica Educational Corporation, 1970. 24 vols.

Encyclopedia of Associations. 6th ed. Detroit, Gale Research, 1970. 3 vols.

International Encyclopedia of the Social Sciences. David L. Sills, ed. New York, Macmillan, 1968. 17 vols.

Lincoln Library of Essential Information. Revised ed. Buffalo, N.Y., Frontier Press, 1968. 1 or 2 vols.

Walsh, S. Padraig, comp. *General Encyclopedias in Print, 1969; A Comparative Analysis.* New York, Bowker, 1969. (Revised annually.)

World Book Encyclopedia. Chicago, Field Enterprises Educational Corporation, 1970. 20 vols.

NEWSPAPERS AND
MAGAZINES

Oɴᴇ of the freedoms is Freedom of Information, a citizen's right to know. He has a right to know serious things like what happens to his taxes, how his representative in Congress is voting, and when and where important meetings are being held. And he has the right to know what new books are published, what plays and movies are opening, and what the ball scores are.

Governments sometimes withhold information and sometimes lie to the people, but in a free society the hope is to keep this to a minimum. The difference between what is withheld or false and what is released and is true is sometimes referred to as the "credibility gap." The idea is to keep the gap from widening.

Newspapers and magazines help inform the public and narrow the credibility gap. Freedom of the Press is the Siamese twin of Freedom of Information. As the citizen has a right to know, the press has a right to tell him.

Newspapers and magazines are especially important sources because they give the most recent information on a subject and give material on subjects too new or perhaps too temporary to be covered in books.

Newspapers and some magazine articles are considered *primary sources*. A primary source is distinguished from a secondary source by the fact that it is an eyewitness account given by someone who participates in events or is present as an observer. A student or researcher, using a number of such primary sources, then produces a paper which is a secondary source. The more removed a researcher gets from primary sources the more likely it is that the information may be distorted in the same way that the message is garbled when whispered from person to person in the game of telephone.

Newspapers and magazines supply you with information today and, through indexes and preservation in such forms as microfilm, supply that information in exactly the same way to your great grandchildren at a later day. Future generations are provided with undiluted history. The interpretation or significance of events may change in the light of history and new knowledge but the basic facts and contemporary reactions are preserved.

MAGAZINES AND MAGAZINE INDEXES.

Magazines are a way of keeping up-to-date and a way of finding various viewpoints on a subject. They're also called "periodicals" because they are issued at regular intervals—every week, every month, four times a year (quarterly), etc. Several issues of a magazine make up a volume. Usually, but not always, a volume number covers a year's issues. Indexes to magazines refer to the name of the magazine, the volume number, page number and date of issue.

Readers' Guide to Periodical Literature

The Readers' Guide is an index to the articles in over one hundred familiar and commonly used magazines. (Some schools and libraries have the *Abridged Readers' Guide,* which is the same except that it indexes fewer magazines.) The magazine articles are indexed by subject and by author in one alphabetical list.

Actually the Readers' Guide is itself a periodical because it is issued in paperback form twice a month. These are eventually "cumulated" or interfiled into one alphabetical list covering longer periods of time and then bound into hardcover books. The covers of the issues and of the bound volumes indicate the time period encompassed (see illustration).

S<small>AMPLE</small> C<small>OVER OF</small> P<small>APERBACK</small> I<small>SSUE OF</small> R<small>EADERS</small>' G<small>UIDE</small>

MAY 25, 1970
Vol. 70   No. 7
Includes indexing from April 17—April 30, 1970

READERS' GUIDE
to periodical literature
(UNABRIDGED)

An index to selected U.S.
general and non-technical
periodicals of reference
value in libraries.

THE H.W.WILSON COMPANY

◄Date index was issued.

◄Period covered by the magazines indexed in Readers' Guide.

Sample spine of bound volume.

Period covered by magazines indexed.►

Readers' Guide volume number.►

READERS' GUIDE
TO
PERIODICAL
LITERATURE

MARCH 1967-
FEBRUARY 1968

27

ABBREVIATIONS OF PERIODICALS INDEXED

March 1967—February 1968

FOR FULL INFORMATION, CONSULT PAGES IX-XI

ALA Bul—ALA Bulletin
Aero Tech—Aerospace Technology
  Formerly Technology Week including
  Missiles and Rockets
Am Artist—American Artist
Am City—American City
Am Ed—American Education
Am For—American Forests
*Am Heritage—American Heritage
Am Hist R—American Historical Review
Am Home—American Home
Am Rec G—American Record Guide
America—America
Américas—Américas
Ann Am Acad—Annals of the American Acad-
  emy of Political and Social Science
Antiques—Antiques
Arch Forum—Architectural Forum
Arch Rec—Architectural Record
Art N—Art News
*Atlan—Atlantic
Audubon—Audubon
Aviation W—Aviation Week & Space Tech-
  nology
Bet Hom & Gard—Better Homes and Gardens
Bsns W—Business Week
Bul Atomic Sci—Bulletin of the Atomic Sci-
  entists

Life—Life
Liv Wildn—Living Wilderness
*Look—Look (Middle Atlantic edition)
McCalls—McCall's
M'lle—Mademoiselle
Mo Labor R—Monthly Labor Review
Mod Phot—Modern Photography
Motor B—Motor Boating
Motor T—Motor Trend

NEA J—NEA Journal
N Y Times Mag—New York Times Magazine
*Nat Geog Mag—National Geographic Magazine
Nat Parks Mag—National Parks Magazine
Nat R—National Review (44p issue only, pub.
  in alternate weeks)
Nation—Nation
Nations Bsns—Nation's Business
*Natur Hist—Natural History Incorporating
  Nature Magazine
Negro Hist Bul—Negro History Bulletin
New Repub—New Republic
New Yorker—New Yorker
*Newsweek—Newsweek

Opera N—Opera News
Outdoor Life—Outdoor Life
PTA Mag—PTA Magazine

ABBREVIATIONS

The entries give the names of the magazines in abbreviated form. The front of the guide has a list of abbreviations used for the periodicals and another list with full bibliographic information for the periodicals indexed in the Readers' Guide. (See illustration.)

LIST OF PERIODICALS INDEXED

All data as of latest issue received

ALA Bulletin—available only to members. m (bi-m Jl-Ag) American Library Association, 50 E Huron St, Chicago 60611

Aerospace Technology—$6. bi-w Aerospace Technology, 1001 Vermont Av, NW, Washington, D.C. 20005
  Formerly Technology Week including Missiles and Rockets

America—$10. w (bi-w year-end issue) America Press, 106 W 56th St, New York 10019

The American Academy of Political and Social Science Annals—$10. free to members. bi-m American Academy of Political and Social Science, 3937 Chestnut St, Philadelphia 19104

American Artist—$8. m (S-Je) American Artist, 2160 Patterson St, Cincinnati, Ohio 45214

The American City—$10. m Buttenheim Pub. Corp, 757 3d Av, New York 10017

American Education—$3.75. m (bi-m D, Jl) American Education, Superintendent of Documents, U.S. Government Printing

Bulletin of the Atomic Scientists—$7. m (S-Je) Bulletin of the Atomic Scientists, 935 E 60th St, Chicago 60637

Business Week—$10. w Business Week, P.O. Box 430, Hightstown, N.J. 08520

The Catholic World—$6. m Catholic World, Harristown Road, Glen Rock, N.J. 07452

*Changing Times—$6. m Changing Times, The Kiplinger Magazine, Editors Park, Md. 20782

The Christian Century—$8.50. w Christian Century Foundation, 407 S Dearborn St, Chicago 60605

Commentary—$9. m American Jewish Committee, 165 E 56th St, New York 10022

Commonweal—$9. w (bi-w year-end issue, mid-Jl-mid-S) Commonweal Pub. Co, Inc, 232 Madison Av, New York 10016

Congressional Digest—$10. m (S-Je) Congressional Digest Corp, 3231 P St, NW, Washington, D.C. 20007

*Consumer Bulletin—$5. m Consumers' Re-

Other abbreviations used are also given in a key at the front of each issue or volume. Those abbreviations used for the months are shown, "il" for illustration, "por" for portrait, etc.

KEY TO ABBREVIATIONS

*	following name entry, a printer's device	jr	junior
+	continued on later pages of same issue	jt auth	joint author
		ltd	limited
abp	archbishop		
abr	abridged	m	monthly
Ag	August	Mr	March
Ap	April	My	May
arch	architect		
assn	association	N	November
Aut	Autumn	no	number
av	avenue		
		O	October
bart	baronet		
bibliog	bibliography	por	portrait
bibliog f	bibliographical foot- notes	pseud	pseudonym
		pt	part
bi-m	bimonthly	pub	published, publisher, publishing
bi-w	biweekly		
bldg	building	q	quarterly
bp	bishop		
		rev	revised
co	company		
comp	compiled, compiler	S	September
cond	condensed	sec	section
cont	continued	semi-m	semimonthly
corp	corporation	soc	society
		Spr	Spring
D	December	sq	square
dept	department	sr	senior
		st	street
ed	edited, edition, editor	Sum	Summer
		sup	supplement
F	February	supt	superintendent
Hon	Honorable		
		tr	translated, transla- tion, translator
il	illustrated, illustra- tion, illustrator		
inc	incorporated	v	volume
introd	introduction, intro- ductory		
		w	weekly
Ja	January	Wint	Winter
Je	June		
Jl	July	yr	year

Sample entry: PHOTOGRAPHY
For better holiday pictures; open your mind first. K. Poll. il Pop Phot 66:78-9+ Ja

Explanation: An illustrated article on the subject PHOTOG- RAPHY entitled "For better holiday pic- tures: open your mind first," by K. Poll, will be found in volume 66 of Popular Photog- raphy, pages 78-9 (continued on later pages of the same issue) the January 1970 number

Sample page from Readers' Guide (reduced)

1088   READERS' GUIDE TO PERIODICAL LITERATURE March 1967–February 1968

SPIDERS, Red. See Red spiders
SPIEGEL, Marshall
    News on wheels. Sr Schol 91:38-9 S 28; 26
    D 14 '67
SPIEGEL, Der. See Periodicals—Germany
    (Federal Republic)
SPIES
    Aeroflot: Soviet spy line? il U S News 62:64
    My 29 '67
    Covey of spies is flushed in Germany. M.
    Durham and J. Cook. il Life 63:65-6+ N 3
    '67
    Espionage establishments; excerpt. D. Wise
    and T. B. Ross. il Sat Eve Post 240:29-31+
    O 21; 50-3+ N 4; 76-80+ N 18 '67
    Lesson of Philby. Nat R 19:1155 O 31 '67
    When a red spymaster defected to U.S. U S
    News 63:11 N 20 '67
    See also
    Espionage
    Loginov, IU.
    Philby, H. A. R.
    Roessler
    Secret service
    Trials (espionage)
    Wynne, G.
SPIES, industrial
    Big corporations can have their own CIA.
    New Repub 156:18 F 18 '67
    Bitten by a bug; chairman of Amphenol corp.
    makes charge of corporate espionage. News-
    week 70:55-6 N 20 '67
    How to steal $4 billion. il Newsweek 69:76-8
    My 1 '67
SPIES and dolls; drama. See Murray, J.
SPIES in literature
    Bond and I; techniques of Ian Fleming; Le
    Delghton; John Le Carré. S. Elmerl. Re-
    porter 37:55-8 Jl 13 '67
    Lucky Jim Bond. il Newsweek 69:61 My 8 '67
    Many lives of James Bond. il Esquire 67:73-85
    Mr '67
SPILHAUS, Athelstan F.
    Geotechnology objectives demand imagina-
    tive planning. por Tech W 20:68-71 Ja 23
    '67
        about
    Cities under glass. il por Newsweek 71:44-5
    Ja 8 '68
    Should U.S. cities be torn down? U S News
    64:10 Ja 8 '68
SPILLER, Burton L.
    Grouse oddities. Field & S 72:46-7+ N '67
SPINAL column. See Spine
SPINAL cord
        Surgery
    Claim of mended spine questioned. Bsns W
    p96 D 2 '67
    Miracle surgery case; dispute over operation
    by G. Murray. il Newsweek 70:56+ D 11 '67
    Rejoining the spinal cord. il Time 90:70 N
    24 '67
    Repairing the paraplegic. il Newsweek 70:66
    N 27 '67
    Spinal cord spliced, paralyzed patient starts
    recovery. Sci N 92:534 D 2 '67
SPINAL curvature. See Spine—Abnormities
    and deformities
SPINDLETOP. See Oil wells
SPINE
    Biped's burden. il Newsweek 70:59 O 16 '67
        Abnormities and deformities
    New heartbreak in Ingrid Bergman's life:
    daughter's illness. M. S. Davis. il Good H
    165:51-2+ N '67
    Slipped disk. Todays Health 45:77-8 Ja '68
SPINELLO, Matt P.
    On the citizens band. See issues of Popular
    electronics
SPINNAKERS. See Sails
SPINNER, Thomas J. Jr
    From defeat to disaster. Nation 204:583-9 My
    8 '67
SPINNING reels. See Fishing tackle
SPINOZA, Benedictus de
    Varieties of Jewish experience. M. Him-
    melfarb. Commentary 44:54-61 Jl '67
SPINRAD, Bernard I.
    New role for the national laboratories; text
    of declaration. Bul Atomic Sci 23:30-1 Ja
    '67
SPINRAD, R. J.
    Automation in the laboratory. Science 158:55-
    60 O 6 '67
SPINS, Airplane. See Airplanes—Spinning
SPINSTERS. See Single women
SPIRACLES (insects) See Respiratory organs
    —Insects
SPIRATONE adapters. See Lenses, Photo-
    graphic

SPIREAS
    Choice creeping shrub. M. Halpin. Home
    Gard 54:14 F '67
SPIRIT. See Soul
SPIRIT, Holy. See Holy Spirit
SPIRITS. See Ghosts
SPIRITS, Photography of. See Photography of
    apparitions
SPIRITUAL life
    See also
    Christian life
SPIRITUAL-mindedness. See Spirituality
SPIRITUAL retreats. See Retreats, Spiritual
SPIRITUALISM
    Medium's message; televised séance with
    Bishop Pike. il Newsweek 70:57 O 9 '67
    Messages through the medium; beliefs of
    Bishop Pike. il Time 90:55 O 6 '67
SPIRITUALITY
    Field concept of spirituality. A. B. Haines.
    Christian Cent 84:1332-4 O 18 '67
SPIRO, Al
    Burning issues. il por Newsweek 70:51 Ag 7
    '67
SPIROGRAPH. See Drawing instruments
SPITBALL pitching. See Pitching (baseball)
SPITTLE insects. See Froghoppers
SPITZ, Mark
    All set to number 1; with report by
    B. Bruns. il por Life 63:47-8+ S 15 '67
    Old and new pool their talent. K. Chapin. por
    Sports Illus 27:48+ Ag 21 '67
    Times came for two teens. K. Chapin. il
    por Sports Illus 26:97-9 Ap 17 '67
SPITZER, David L.
    Hoffa taint. New Repub 156:5 Je 10 '67
SPITZER, Elroy F.
    Cities play a major role in eutrophication.
    Am City 82:99+ Ag '67
    Continuous ion-exchange softening. Am City
    82:118-20 Je '67
    Which trees and what street surfacing. Am
    City 82:97+ Jl '67
SPITZER, Helen. See Spitzer, S. jt. auth.
SPITZER, Maurice
    Doctor Maurice Spitzer: pioneer of the
    Judaic book art. I. Solfer. il Pub W 192:
    83-4+ S 4 '67
SPITZER, Richard C.
    Today's Catholic schools. Cath World 206:167-
    70 Ja '68
SPITZER, Silas
    Dining in Chicago. Holiday 41:84-6+ Mr '67
    Finest food of France. Holiday 42:70-1+ N
    '67
    Good soup. Holiday 42:74-7+ O '67
    —and Spitzer, Helen
    Holiday's choice of American restaurants.
    Holiday 42:99-104 Jl '67
SPIVACK, G. J. See Julesz, B. jt. auth.
SPIVACK, Kathleen
    Fat-lipped, you formless; poem. Atlan 220:91
    Jl '67
SPIVAK, Lawrence E.
    Making news with a news show. il por Sr
    Schol 91:5 N 2 '67
SPLEEN cells. See Cells
SPLICERS, Television. See Couplings, Electric
SPLICES. See Knots and splices
SPLICING amateur moving pictures. See Mov-
    ing pictures, Amateur—Editing
SPLICING of moving pictures. See Moving
    pictures—Editing
SPLIT-level houses. See Architecture, Domestic
SPOCK, Benjamin
    Children must be protected from the harm
    of race. Negro Hist Bul 30:14 Ap '67
    First hours. Redbook 130:65-71+ N '67
    How children learn the joy of giving. por
    Redbook 129:41-3+ S '67
    (Monthly column) See issues of Redbook
    —and Hathaway, M. L.
    Montessori and traditional American nursery
    schools, how they are different, how they
    are alike. por Redbook 128.20+ Mr '67
        about
    Doctor's dilemma. il por Time 91:14-15 Ja 12
    '68
    Law and Dr Spock. Newsweek 71:18+ Ja
    15 '68
    Peace, man, says baby doctor Spock. R.
    Reeves. il por N Y Times Mag p8-9+ Jl 16
    '67
    SANE warning. Christian Cent 84:1419-20 N
    8 '67; Reply. R. J. Neuhaus. 84:1600 D 13
    '67
SPOFFORD; drama. See Shumlin, H.

Ringed entries enlarged and explained

Subject Entry

SPIES
Aeroflot: Soviet spy line? il U S News 62:64
My 29 '67
Covey of spies is flushed in Germany. M.
Durham and J. Cook. il Life 63:65-6+ N 3

"See Also" References to
Related Material

Lesson of Philby. Nat R 19:1155 O 31 '67
When a red spymaster defected to U.S. U S
News 63:11 N 20 '67
—See also

Bitten by a bug; chairman of Amphenol corp.
makes charge of corporate espionage. Newsweek 70:85-6 N 20 '67

Illustrated Article

How to steal $4 billion. [il] Newsweek 69:76-8
My 1 '67

Newsweek Magazine, Vol-
ume 71, Pages 44-45, January 8, 1968.

about

Cities under glass. il por Newsweek 71:44-5
Ja 8 '68
Should U.S. cities be torn down? U S News
64:10 Ja 8 '68

Abnormities and deformities———————— Subheading

New heartbreak in Ingrid Bergman's life;
daughter's illness. M. S. Davis. il Good H
161:54-7+ Ja '67
Slipped disk. Todays Health 46:77-8 Ja '68

Author Entry ——————— **SPINNER, Thomas J. Jr**
From defeat to disaster. Nation 204:588-9 My
8 '67

SPIRIT. See Soul
SPIRIT, Holy. See Holy Spirit
SPIRITS. See Ghosts
SPIRITS, Photography of. See Photography of
apparitions
SPIRITUAL life

"See" References from
Headings Not Used to
Headings Used.

Portrait of Person in News
Story Is Included in Illustrations.

SPIRO, Al
Burning issues. il por Newsweek 70:51 Ag 7
'67
SPIROGRAPH. See Drawing instruments

SPITZ, Mark
All out to be number 1; with report by
B. Bruns. il pors Life 63:47-8+ S 15 '67
Old and new pool their talent. K. Chapin. por
Sports Illus 27:48+ Ag 21 '67

Sports Illustrated, Volume
26, pages 97-99, April 17,
1967

Times came for two teens. K. Chapin. il
por Sports Illus 26:97-9 Ap 17 '67

SPOCK, Benjamin
Children must be protected from the harm
of race. Negro Hist Bul 30:14 Ap '67
First hours. Redbook 130:65-71+ N '67
How children learn the joy of giving. por
Redbook 129:41-3+ S '67
[Monthly column] See issues of Redbook
—and Hathaway. M. L.
Montessori and traditional American nursery
schools; how they are different; how they
are alike. por Redbook 128.20+ Mr '67

"By and About" Articles

about

Doctor's dilemma. il por Time 91:14-15 Ja 12
'68
Law and Dr Spock. Newsweek 71:18+ Ja
15 '68

Title Entry (Referring to
Main Entry Under Author's
Name)

SPOFFORD; drama. See Shumlin, H.

See sample page for illustrations of the following:

CROSS REFERENCES

When you do not find any articles named under a subject heading you will usually find an instruction to look under another heading. This is called a "see reference"—from a heading not used to the heading used.

Under some subjects you will find "see also references." These are reminders to look at related subject headings which might also have articles useful to you.

SUBHEADINGS

If the subject is very broad and there are many entries, it will be divided by "subheadings." These break down a subject into smaller, specific aspects. They are printed in the middle of the column, instead of at the left side as the main headings are. A particularly important subhead used under several subjects is "Criticisms, plots, etc." This subheading will help you locate reviews under such headings as "Operas," "Dramas," and "Moving picture plays."

BY AND ABOUT REFERENCES

Sometimes there will be two alphabetical listings under a famous person's name. The first is a list of articles *by* the person as author and the second is a list of articles *about* the person.

TITLES

Titles of articles are *not* in the index but titles of stories appear with a "see reference" to the author's name for full information.

There are some other periodical indexes which, though available only in larger reference libraries, are worth knowing about for special use. *Poole's Index* indexes English and American periodicals from 1802 to 1907 and the *Nineteenth Century Readers' Guide* covers the period from 1890 to about 1922. (The *Readers' Guide to Periodical Literature* covers the Twentieth Century.) Poole's, by the way, was started by a student, William Frederick Poole, who saw the need for it while studying at Yale.

Other indexes are limited to periodicals on special subjects such as: *Biological and Agricultural Index, Applied Science and Technology Index, Art Index, Business Periodicals Index, Catholic Periodicals Index, Education Index,* and *Social Sciences and Humanities Index.* These are set up and used in generally the same way as the Readers' Guide.

In addition to finding information *in* magazines, there are ways of finding out *about* them. There are directories which list periodicals according to subject (medicine, education, sports, etc.) and give information on subscriptions, circulation and related material. The *Standard Periodical Directory* lists U.S. and Canadian periodicals and *Ulrich's International Periodicals Directory* is a very comprehensive world list in two volumes.

NEWSPAPERS

Journalist Walter Lippmann gave this definition of a newspaper's responsibility: "To bring to light the hidden facts, to set them into relation with each other, to make a picture of reality on which men can act."

It is that "picture of reality" written by a man on the scene that makes a newspaper a primary source for current history and, through back issues, brings "ancient" history to life.

Notice certain things when you're reading the newspaper. Look at the *dateline* because it translates any use of the words "here" and "today" in the story. The dateline will indicate if "here" means your hometown or Moscow and it will tell you if "today" means yesterday and not the date on which the newspaper is issued (especially possible in the case of a morning paper). And notice the *source*. The story may be written by a local or foreign reporter (and given a *by-line*) or by a *wire service*. A newspaper cannot afford to have reporters at every national and international news event so it buys the services of larger news gathering organizations called wire services.

(Samples from *New York Times*, Feb. 25, 1970)

POLLUTION EBBING IN CITY'S WATERS

12 Treatment Plants Now Process 75% of Sewage

By BAYARD WEBSTER
Although oil seepage, noxious

By-line of local reporter and current story so no place or date given.

By-line of reporter in another city covering events which took place day before newspaper's date of issue.

EX-U.S. AIDES URGE BONDS IN CHICAGO

Clark, Marshall Sign Brief Drawn Up by the A.C.L.U.

By JOHN KIFNER
Special to The New York Times
CHICAGO, Feb. 24—Ramsey Clark, the former Attoney Gen-

Tito and Nasser End Talks

ASWAN, United Arab Republic, Feb. 24 (AP)—President Tito of Yugoslavia and President Gamal Abdel Nasser held their second of two sessions on the Middle East crisis today.

Dateline indicates Aswan events of day before and it is taken from a wire service (AP) which stands for the Associated Press.

Some awareness of how news stories are written is helpful. The pattern of most news stories is almost the reverse of the pattern in fiction. That is, the news story, instead of building to a climax, begins with a condensation of the climax or the important aspects of the event. It then proceeds to present the facts in descending order of importance. This formula saves the reader time. If, after reading the first few paragraphs, you have the information you're looking for you need not read on, but if it is a subject about which you need to know all pertinent facts they are there for you. A headline is a further abbreviation of the story.

The front page will also tell you what edition you're reading. If there is a lot of developing news, a paper will print several editions in one day to keep the stories up-to-date. The later the edition, the more complete the information given.

Some newspapers are, of course, better than others. Good newspapers offer background articles, pictures, maps, and analysis in addition to an account of the event. A good newspaper keeps opinion out of the news columns and reserves it for the editorial page where it can be recognized as opinion. Advertisers should not have any influence over the news and editorials.

Libraries keep back files of local newspapers, some of which are preserved on microfilm. Most newspapers do not have detailed indexes available to the public but the *New York Times Index*, described below, is very useful in locating material in other newspapers because it gives a clue to the date of events.

HOW TO USE THE NEW YORK TIMES INDEX

The Index is the only service that presents a condensed, classified history of the world as it is recorded day-by-day in The New York Times. It consists of abstracts of news and editorial matter (*entries*) entered under appropriate headings. Headings and their subdivisions, if any, are arranged alphabetically; the entries under them are arranged chronologically. Each entry is followed by a precise reference—date, page and column—to the item which it summarizes. All related headings are covered either by cross-references or by duplicate entries.

SOURCE: The Index encompasses the news and editorial matter in the final Late City Edition of The Times—the same edition that is microfilmed—including the Sunday supplementary sections and including advertisements that are related to the news and likely to be of interest to users. Material is omitted only when it is of such transitory interest as to have no discernible research value.

HEADINGS: Whenever possible, entries are made under "subject" headings (e.g., Agriculture, Housing, Steel). Under geographic headings will be found, usually, only material on the government, general defenses, finances, economy, politics and social conditions of the country; i.e., material too broad to fit under subject headings. Names of persons and organizations are usually covered by cross-references to the subjects of their activities. Entries are made under the most specific heading (e.g., material on the steel industry under Steel, and not under Metals), except where the amount of material is too small or where it is advantageous to collect related material under a single heading. Book reviews, deaths, news of art, crime, entertainment and sports, letters to the editor and some other types of news are generally indexed under subject headings only.

Alphabetization: Headings are alphabetized on the word-by-word basis (New York before Newark). Inverted headings precede uninverted headings (New York, State Univ. of, before New York State). Headings beginning with a prefix are treated as though the prefix were a part of the next word (Pan American after Panama). Abbreviated headings appear alphabetically (CIT before Citizens), not at the start of each letter.

Inversions: Multiple-word headings are inverted if a word other than the first is deemed to be the "key word" in identifying the heading (e.g.,United Steelworkers of America to Steelworkers of America, United). Personal names containing a prefix are entered under the prefix if the person is an American or British national (e.g., de Mille, Agnes), and usually under the word following the prefix for other nationalities (e.g., Gaulle, Charles de). An effort is made to observe national or personal preferences whenever they can be ascertained.

SUBDIVISIONS: Headings are subdivided whenever the amount of material entered there warrants it and the nature of the material permits. Subdivisions consist of **Main Subheads** (set thus in bold-face type) and, where further subdivision is necessary, of *Secondary Subheads* (set thus in italics and preceded by a bullet subhead ●). Both types of subheads are arranged alphabetically. Material that does not lend itself to classification under subheads appears directly under the main heading. Material that does not lend itself to classification under secondary subheads appears directly under the main subhead.

ENTRIES: Entries are by no means limited to a minimal indication of the general content of the item from which they derive; to the contrary, they seek to present concisely all the significant material which is pertinent under a given heading. Entries are made under all headings where the item may be pertinent and which are not covered by appropriate cross-references, and sometimes in addition to such cross-references.

Entries appear in chronological order except in

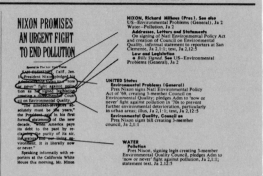

listings under Book Reviews, Deaths, Theater-Reviews, and the like, where an alphabetical arrangement is clearly preferable.

Entries for closely related material may be grouped into paragraphs. Where two or more such paragraphs appear, they are arranged chronologically as determined by the date reference of the first entry in each paragraph. (In cross-references to entries in such paragraphs, the paragraphs are identified by the date of their first entry. For example, "Ja 5 in Ja 2 par" refers to an entry dated January 5 contained in a paragraph beginning with an entry dated January 2.)

When a news story is accompanied by the text or transcript of official statements or documents, or by photographs, cartoons, maps, graphs or other illustrative material, the entries specify that such material is included.

Entries of unusual interest are set in bold-face type. Under headings containing a large number of entries, these bold-face entries are useful guideposts in the search for an item whose date the reader may not know.

DATE, PAGE, COLUMN REFERENCES: Each entry concludes with the date, page and column of the story's publication in The Times (e.g., My 1, 1:8 means that the story was published on May 1, page 1, column 8). Sunday sections other than the main news sections are identified by Roman numerals following the date (e.g., in My 6, IV, 3:4 the numeral IV denotes the News of the Week in Review section).

If an entry summarizes a news story which begins on one page and continues on another, the reference is to the page on which the story begins. If an entry summarizes material found only in the continuation, the reference is to the page of the continuation, and not to the beginning of the story.

Since most international, national and general news now appears everywhere almost simultaneously, the date references indicate when the news may have appeared in other publications. However, The Index cannot be used to obtain *precise* references to other publications or to editions of The Times other than the final Late City Edition. The reader is also cautioned that the date references in The Index denote the dates of publication in The Times, and not the dates of the events themselves.

CROSS-REFERENCES: Cross-references are arranged in alphabetical order, except that cross-references

to general categories of headings (e.g., Food. See ...food names) usually follow the more specific ones. Cross-references guiding to a single entry under another heading will show not only the heading or subhead where that entry is located but also the date of the entry if necessary.

Cross-references do not indicate the specific content of the entries to which they refer, and should not be so construed. Thus a cross-reference from a person's name to a crime heading cannot and does not indicate whether that person is a defendant, a witness, a prosecutor, or a person merely commenting on the subject but not a party to it.

Many terms are cross-referenced to headings where these terms are used as subheads. Sometimes the cross-reference does not spell out the subhead, when it is obvious, but leaves it implied. (For example: Accidents. See also Airlines. Under the heading Airlines, a subhead Accidents and Safety will be found.)

Sometimes cross-references are made from names of persons or organizations to entries in which these names are not brought out but implied. Thus the entry "school and board representatives comment on budget" would be applicable to any person from whose name a reference to this entry had been made.

Cross references are made from country names to United Nations and to other international organizations of which the given country is a member. Such cross-references are intended to cover, at times implicitly, the country's participation in all of the organization's activities, whether these are indexed by entries under the organization directly, or by cross-references from the organization's name to subjects.

In conformity with standard library practice, a "see" cross-reference is used when the heading from which it runs is not open for entries and the heading to which it leads is used in preference. "See also" cross-references guide from headings that may be opened for entries to other headings where relevant material is entered.

ADDENDA AND ERRATA: Corrections for current and earlier volumes appear in the back of each Annual. Corrections are also printed when necessary in the back of semi-monthly issues. The publishers wish to make The Index as accurate as possible, and will be grateful if subscribers will bring to their attention any inaccuracies they may find.

The above instructions appear in each issue of *The New York Times Index.*

THE NEW YORK TIMES INDEX

This index is briefly described here because, though it may not be available in your school library, the index and the newspaper on microfilm are available in public and university libraries across the United States. And, as mentioned, the *New York Times Index* is useful in locating items in your local papers (except, of course, strictly local-interest events) because it establishes dates.

The reasons for the availability of *The New York Times* are that it goes far back in time (it began in 1851), it has been preserved on microfilm and carefully indexed for most of its long life, it has a reputation for reliability and accuracy because it sees itself as a "newspaper of record." And, to risk boasting, some of the finest editors and writers form its staff—a claim supported by thirty-six Pulitzer Prizes (annual awards for outstanding achievement in journalism). *The New York Times* also often prints the *full text* of items that are only described in other papers and magazines. The index, under the subject entry, indicates by the words "text" or "excerpts" or "transcript" (for a news conference, etc.) what you will find in the newspaper.

Here is the "How to Use The New York Times Index" page from an index volume. It is best to review this page before using the index.

Though the *New York Times Index* is much more complex, there are similarities between it and the Readers' Guide. Both have "see" and "see also" references, subheads under major headings, and abbreviations are defined in the front of the indexes.

The references are to the date of the newspaper in which the story appears (not necessarily the date of the event), the page number and the column number. A page has eight columns, numbered 1 on the extreme left to 8 on the far right. If the article appeared in a Sunday paper a section number (in Roman numerals) may also be given.

Ja 11, 1:5   This refers to a story which appeared in the paper of January 11th, on page one, column five.

My 1, VI, 33   This refers to a story which appeared on May 1st, in section six—the Magazine—on page thirty-three. No column number is given because the format of this section of the Sunday paper is different from that of the news section. (*The New York Times Magazine* is also indexed in the Readers' Guide because, though part of a newspaper, it is considered a periodical in its own right.)

The Times' index is published twice a month and then cumulated into a single volume for each year.

One of the special aspects of the *New York Times Index* is that it can be used as a reference tool by itself without necessarily continuing on to the newspaper story. Major news stories are given *brief summaries* in the index and entries are *listed chronologically* under the subject so the course of events is clearly seen. The most *important events are easily identified by black bold type.* Since 1965 the index has included graphs, pictures, maps and other illustrative material. Here is an example from the 1968 index:

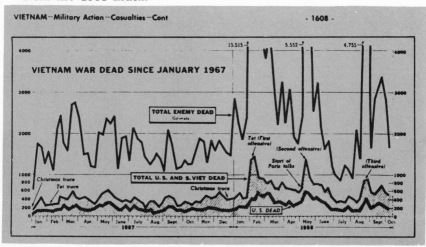

The index all by itself is valuable for finding the names and the spelling of new nations and newly elected officials, and for finding sports records, statistics, dates and the meanings of current initials. Under "Deaths" you'll find a list of prominent persons who have died in a given year; there are other important collective headings such as "Book reviews." (Some of these collective headings are indicated under appropriate subjects in this guide.)

In the unlikely event that the name of one of the Beatles escapes you, a quick check in the Times' index under "Beatles" will show all four names—provided, of course, it's the index for a year when the Beatles were in the news. This is from the 1967 index:

> **BEATLES, The (George Harrison, John Lennon, Paul McCartney, Ringo Starr). See also** Apparel—GB, N 21. Drug Addiction Jl 25. Motion Pictures—Revs, How I Won the War. Music Jl 25. Music—Awards Mr 27. TV—GB, D 27,28 ▲ Lennon illus, Ja 15,II, 13:2; McCartney says group is breaking up, int, Ja 23,29:1; their mgr B Epstein dies, Ag 28,31:4 (**see also** Epstein, B); they postpone pilgrimage to India, to study with mystic, in order to complete 1-hr TV special; 3 say they have stopped taking drugs, S 11,53:1

As with all reference sources, the best way to familiarize yourself with *The New York Times Index* is to look up a subject you know about and see how it is handled. Become acquainted with the newspaper by looking at the microfilm for the day you were born and see what other important events took place that memorable day. Even the advertisements will help reveal that segment of the past.

There also exist ways of finding information *about* newspapers as well as *in* them. There are two major directories which list newspapers by state and then city, giving publishers, editors, circulation, etc. They are the *Editor and Publisher International Yearbook* and *N. W. Ayer and Son's Directory of Newspapers and Periodicals.*

BIBLIOGRAPHY: MAGAZINE AND NEWS-PAPER INDEXES

Applied Science and Technology Index. New York, H. W. Wilson, 1958 to date. Monthly except Aug. Annual cumulations.

Art Index. New York, H. W. Wilson, 1929 to date. Quarterly with cumulations.

Biological and Agricultural Index. New York, H. W. Wilson, 1964 to date. Monthly except Sept. Cumulated. (Prior to 1964 was called *Agricultural Index*, 1916—.)

Business Periodicals Index. New York, H. W. Wilson, 1958 to date. Monthly except July. Annual cumulations.

Catholic Periodical Index. Villanova, Pa., Catholic Library Association, 1930 to date. Quarterly. Two-year cumulations.

Editor and Publisher International Yearbook. New York, Editor and Publisher, 1920 to date. Annual.

Education Index. New York, H. W. Wilson, 1929 to date. Monthly except July and August. Cumulations.

N. W. Ayer and Son's Directory of Newspapers and Periodicals. Philadelphia, N. W. Ayer, 1880 to date.

New York Times Index. New York, New York Times, 1913 to date. Semimonthly. Annual cumulations.

Nineteenth Century Readers' Guide to Periodical Literature. New York, H. W. Wilson, 1944. 2 vols.

Poole's Index to Periodical Literature. Boston, Houghton Mifflin, 1882. 2 vols. Five supplements, 1887-1908.

Readers' Guide to Periodical Literature. New York, H. W. Wilson, 1900 to date. Semi-monthly except monthly in July and August. Cumulations.

Social Sciences and Humanities Index. New York, H. W. Wilson, 1916 to date. Quarterly with cumulations. (Formerly called *International Index.*)

Standard Periodical Directory, 1970. 3rd ed. New York, Oxbridge, 1969.

Ulrich's International Periodicals Directory, 1969-70. 13th ed. New York, Bowker, 1969. 2 vols.

PART TWO

Reference Books In Subject Areas

ART

BOOKS AND LITERATURE

BUSINESS, ECONOMICS AND STATISTICS

CUSTOMS AND HOLIDAYS

EDUCATION

GEOGRAPHY

HISTORY

INDUSTRIAL ARTS

MATHEMATICS

MUSIC

MYTHOLOGY

PARLIAMENTARY PROCEDURE

PHILOSOPHY AND RELIGION

PLAYS

POETRY

POLITICS, GOVERNMENT AND CURRENT EVENTS

QUOTATIONS

SCIENCE

SPEECHES

SPORTS, RECREATION AND HOBBIES

ART

Aʀᴛ has been described as an imitation of nature and as a lie which makes us realize the truth. One work of art is a photograph of the "Mona Lisa" upon which a moustache has been drawn. Both this and the original painting are concerned with art. In a diverse subject, filled with contradictions, it is well that there are some excellent books.

Gardner, Helen. *Art Through the Ages*. 4th ed. rev. Ed. by Sumner M. Crosby. Harcourt, Brace & World, 1959.

Gardner's is a one-volume survey beginning with ancient art and concluding with material on modern art. It has a glossary of technical terms, many illustrations, and bibliographies at the end of chapters. Here the reader can find an explanation for Marcel Duchamp's Mona Lisa with a moustache. He meant it not as a defacement but as a witty attack on those he felt had betrayed the ideals of art. As daddy of the Dada movement in art, he was dramatizing the view that art had become too precious and too expensive. Years later he signed an unaltered print of the Mona Lisa, subtitling it "Rasée." French for "shaved."

Encyclopedia of World Art. New York, McGraw-Hill, 1959-1968. 15 vols.

This is a collection of scholarly, monographic articles and detailed bibliographies. The last part of each volume is made up of black and white and color plates that are especially good. The index volume is essential for small topics within larger ones. The preface states that the work covers "architecture, sculpture, and painting, and every other man-made object that, regardless of its purpose or technique, enters the field of esthetic judgment because of its form or decoration." An example of this thorough treatment may be found under the heading "Table And Food." Here is a discussion of tableware and accessories both as art in their own right and as depicted in famous paintings with a list of the plate numbers for reproductions of the painting. It includes cross references to articles on "Ceramics" and "Silverware."

Reinach, Salomon. *Apollo.* Rev. ed. New York, Scribner, 1935.

This is an out-of-print guide, probably not found in school libraries, but it's important to know it exists. Chapters are devoted to the significant art periods to the end of the 19th century. It is an English translation of French lectures originally given at the Louvre and it is illustrated. Here we are given another definition of art:

> "A work of art differs in one essential characteristic from those products of human activity which supply the immediate wants of life. Let us consider a palace, a picture. The palace might be merely a very large house, and yet provide satisfactory shelter. Here, the element of art is 'superadded' to that of utility. In a statue, a picture, utility is no longer apparent. The element of art is 'isolated.'"

Janson, Horst Woldemar, and Janson, Dora Jane. *History of Art;* a survey of the major visual arts from the dawn of history to the present day. New York, Abrams, 1962.

A handsomely illustrated work which summarizes Western painting, sculpture and architecture.

Larousse Encyclopedia of Modern Art, From 1800 to the Present Day. General ed., René Huyghe. New York, Prometheus Press, 1965.

One of a series also translated from the French which includes *Larousse Encyclopedia of Prehistoric and Ancient Art* (1962), *Larousse Encyclopedia of Byzantine and Medieval Art* (1963), *Larousse Encyclopedia of Renaissance and Baroque Art* (1964). These books show the art of the period in relation to philosophy, literature, science and social and economic conditions. Illustrated.

Craven, Thomas. *The Rainbow Book of Art.* Cleveland, World, 1956.

Simpler than the others listed here, this is still a useful general book about art. Here, for example, is a reminder that there is more in the painting of the Mona Lisa than the smile: "The background is a greenish-blue vista of shadowy peaks and a winding stream." Illustrated.

Monro, Isabel S., and Monro, Kate M. *Index to Reproductions of American Paintings and First Supplement.* New York, Wilson, 1948, 1964. *Index to Reproductions of European Paintings.* New York, Wilson, 1956.

These indexes help to locate illustrations of paintings in books and exhibition catalogs. Paintings are listed by artist, title of the painting and by subject. When known, the location of the original is given.

Hamlin, Talbot Faulkner. *Architecture Through The Ages.* Rev. ed. New York, Putnam, 1953.

This illustrated work is an excellent survey of architecture from a social point of view. This history of what has been called the "art of the use of space" covers primitive and classical architecture and architecture into the first half of the 20th century. Here is a sample:

These attractive Gothic churches were, all of them, content with lath-and-plaster vaults. In them the last connections between building methods and building form disappeared, and in their very success they did much to establish in America the disastrous separation between engineering

112. INEXPENSIVE WOODEN COUNTRY CHURCH. Richard Upjohn, architect. (*Upjohn's Rural Architecture.*)

and architecture which was to curse American building for two generations. The best of the American Gothic work remains in its simpler, its less ostentatious, monuments: the little churches in which wood was allowed frankly to be itself, as in the small frame chapels which Upjohn designed for country villages and distant mission stations; and the frank carpenter-Gothic of the picturesque high-gabled cottages which rose so bewitchingly embowered in heavy trees along many of our Eastern village streets.

Hitchcock, H. R. and others. *World Architecture*. New York, McGraw-Hill, 1963.

A one volume work which is well illustrated—everything from a diagram of the Parthenon roof construction, pyramids and ziggurats to Frank Lloyd Wright's Guggenheim Museum in New York and Charles Eames' Case Study House in Santa Monica.

American Art Directory. New York, Bowker. Triennial since 1952.

Originally called *American Art Annual*, this work lists museums, art organizations, university art departments, art magazines, art scholarships and fellowships and other miscellaneous current information on art.

Art Index, a cumulative author and subject index to a selected list of fine arts periodicals. New York, Wilson, 1933 to date. Quarterly with cumulations.

Found in larger reference libraries, this cumulative index is a sort of *Readers' Guide* to art magazines, museum bulletins and art annuals. It includes painting, sculpture, archaeology, architecture, ceramics and the graphic arts.

BIOGRAPHY

Though most of the works listed in this category include biographical information on artists, there are many individual biographies and biographical dictionaries covering artists, including many translations from French and Italian originals. Examples of titles covering artists are:

Cummings, Paul. *A Dictionary of Contemporary American Artists*. New York, St. Martin's Press, 1966.

American Federation of Arts. *Who's Who in American Art*. Ed. by Dorothy B. Gilbert. New York, Bowker, 1970. Triennial.

Canaday, John. *Lives of the Painters.* New York, Norton, 1969. 4 vols.

COSTUME

Costume and dress are usually considered art and books on the subject are included with art. Because they also reflect a specific era, they are sometimes included in the history section.

Davenport, Millia. *The Book of Costume.* New York, Crown, 1948. 2 vols.

The Davenport costume book is a chronological survey from early times to the end of the American Civil War. It is profusely illustrated.

Monro, Isabel S. and Cook, Dorothy E. *Costume Index.* Supplement, ed. by I. S. Monro and K. M. Monro. New York, Wilson, 1937, 1957.

Locates plates and pictures of costumes in books and covers all historical periods and almost all nationalities and classes.

Evans, Mary. *Costume Throughout the Ages.* 3rd ed. Philadelphia, Lippincott, 1950. il.

Includes historical dress as shown in early art and continues through the period of World War II. The second part of the book deals with national costumes of all countries. There are those who believe dress is pretty far out today but it's plain compared to some other times. Here is a description of the garb of Charles II:

> "the king and his cavaliers clothed in short doublets, much like modern Eton jackets, displaying generously the fine linen shirt bloused about the waist; in full, be-ribboned rhingraves (a kind of breeches); in low, square-toed shoes with high red heels, and stiff ends of ribbon at the instep; with long stockings of bright silk and a jeweled ribbon garter about the right knee; and in broad-brimmed stiff hats with a profusion of feathers."

BOOKS AND
LITERATURE

T HE FIRST WORKS given below identify, list, or classify all
published books. The other reference works in this section deal
with literature—literature here meaning writing of recognized
quality which expresses ideas of permanent and universal
interest.

A bibliography is a list of books. Bibliographies are available in most fields and can be as brief as three or four listed
books at the end of a short encyclopedia article or as long as
several hundred items. They are useful when a reader wants
to find out about a book—the publisher, the author's name—
or as an aid in the selection of a book for a specific purpose.
The list below is short and general. Excluded here, the reader
will be happy to learn, are books about books about books, or
bibliographies of bibliographies.

United States Catalog. 4th ed. New York, Wilson, 1928; and the
Cumulative Book Index. New York, Wilson, 1933 to date.

The *U.S. Catalog,* listing all books in print on January 1,
1928, is supplemented and brought up to date by the new title,
the *Cumulative Book Index.* Together these two sources list
practically every book printed in the U.S. as well as books published in English in foreign countries. For books too recent to
have appeared in C.B.I., current issues of the periodical *Publishers' Weekly* can be consulted. There is also a publication,
Forthcoming Books, a bimonthly, which lists books not yet in
print.

Publishers' Trade List Annual. New York, Publishers' Weekly, 1873 to date.

This is a collection of publishers' catalogs arranged alphabetically under the names of the publishers. The index volumes to these are:

Books In Print. New York, Bowker. 1948 to date. 2 Vols. Annual. An index by author and title of the books listed in PTLA.

Subject Guide to books in Print. New York, Bowker, 1957 to date. 2 Vols. Annual. A companion volume to Books In Print listing the books by subject. It does not include poetry, fiction or drama.

Paperbound Books in Print. New York, Bowker, 1955 to date.

This is an author/title index to all current paperback books. It is issued monthly with quarterly cumulations, which include a subject guide (exclusive of fiction).

GENERAL LITERATURE

These are especially interesting reference sources because they're filled with information which reflects not only literary history but also the history of civilization. Besides helping to locate and evaluate books and authors, these sources will explain allusions in literature, poetry and lively conversation. Such allusions are to characters, places or events and bring, in a few words, instant recognition and understanding. To be called a Scrooge, is immediately comprehensible to any reader of "A Christmas Carol" because Dickens took many pages and great talent to create him.

Benet, William Rose. *The Reader's Encyclopedia.* 2nd ed. New York, Crowell, 1965.

This one volume work contains (in dictionary arrangement) an amazing amount of information on books, literary characters and terms, and authors. If you're called a "Babbit" or a "Yahoo," a quick check here will explain the term. Also included are references in the fields of art, music and mythology. A glance down page 591 indicates the variety.

There are entries on:

> The Little Foxes, a play
> Little John, the Robin Hood character
> Little Lord Fauntleroy, a children's story
> Little magazines, a discussion of them
> Little Orphan Annie, the poem, now comic strip

There are two excellent companion books: *The Reader's Encyclopedia of American Literature* (New York, Crowell, 1962) and *The Reader's Encyclopedia of Shakespeare* (New York, Crowell, 1966). See full annotation under Plays.

Cambridge History of English Literature. Cambridge, University Press, 1907-32. 15 vols.

This set is a most authoritative, important general history of literature, covering the subject from the earliest times to the end of the 19th century. Written by specialists, it is in chapter form and indexed. A companion set is *The Cambridge History of American Literature* (New York, Putnam, 1917-21. 3 vols.)

Harvey, Sir Paul. *The Oxford Companion to English Literature.* 4th ed. New York, Oxford University Press, 1967.

Harvey, Sir Paul. *The Oxford Companion to Classical Literature.* Oxford, Clarendon Press, 1937.

Hart, James D. *The Oxford Companion to American Literature.* 4th ed. New York, Oxford University Press, 1965.

The Oxford Companions are one-volume works and all follow the general format of a dictionary in their alphabetical arrangement. They are reliable and thorough and often include related articles such as one on censorship in the Companion to English Literature. In the back of the Companion to American Literature there is a chronological index showing literary history and social history side by side. Thus a reader can see at a glance that Hemingway's *Farewell to Arms* and Thomas Wolfe's *Look Homeward, Angel* appeared in 1929 when the stock market collapsed and the depression began.

The Cambridge Histories and the Oxford Companions are often confused. Here is an example of how John Donne is treated in a chapter in one volume of a set in the Cambridge History and, on the next page, in a brief dictionary entry in the Oxford Companion:

CHAPTER XI

John Donne

FROM the time of Wyatt, Surrey and their contemporaries of the court of Henry VIII, English lyrical and amatory poetry flowed continuously in the Petrarchian channel. The tradition which these "novices newly crept out of the schools of Dante, Ariosto and Petrarch" brought from Italy, after languishing for some years, was revived and reinvigorated by the influence of Ronsard and Desportes. Spenser in *The Shepheards Calender*, Watson with his pedantic ΕΚΑΤΟΜΠΑΘΙΑ and Sidney with the gallant and passionate sonnets to Stella, led the way; and thereafter, till the publication of Davidson's *Poetical Rapsody*, in 1602, and, subsequently, in the work of such continuers of an older tradition as Drummond, the poets, in sonnet sequence or pastoral eclogue and lyric, told the same tale, set to the same tune. Of the joy of love, the deep contentment of mutual passion, they have little to say (except in some of the finest of Shakespeare's sonnets to his unknown friend), but much of its pains and sorrows—the sorrow of absence, the pain of rejection, the incomparable beauty of the lady and her unwavering cruelty. And they say it in a series of constantly recurring images: of rain and wind, of fire and ice, of storm and warfare; comparisons

> With sun and moon, and earth and sea's rich gems,
> With April's first born flowers and all things rare,
> That heaven's air in this huge rondure hems;

DONNE, JOHN (1571 or 1572–1631), the son of a London ironmonger and of a daughter of J. Heywood (q.v.) the author, was educated both at Oxford and Cambridge, and was entered at Lincoln's Inn. He was in the early part of his life a Roman Catholic. He was secretary to Sir T. Egerton, keeper of the great seal from 1598 to 1602, but alienated his favour by a secret marriage with Anne More, niece of the lord keeper's wife. He sailed in the two expeditions of Essex, to Cadiz and to the Islands, in 1596 and 1597, an episode of which we have a reflection in his early poems 'The Storm' and 'The Calm'. He took Anglican orders in 1615 and preached sermons which rank among the best of the 17th cent. From 1621 to his death he was dean of St. Paul's and frequently preached before Charles I.

In verse he wrote satires, epistles, elegies, and miscellaneous poems, distinguished by wit, profundity of thought and erudition, passion, and subtlety, coupled with a certain roughness of form ('I sing not Syren-like to tempt; for I am harsh'). He was the greatest of the writers of 'metaphysical' poetry, in which passion is interwoven with reasoning. Among his more important poems is the satirical 'Progresse of the Soule', begun in 1601, in which, adopting the doctrine of metempsychosis, he traces the migration of the soul of Eve's apple through the bodies of various heretics. But he left the work uncompleted. His best-known poems are some of the miscellaneous ones, 'The Ecstasie', 'Hymn to God the Father', the sonnet to Death ('Death, be not proud'), 'Go and catch a falling star', etc. They include also a fine funeral elegy (in 'Anniversaries') on the death of Elizabeth Drury, and an 'Epithalamium' on the marriage of the Count Palatine and the Princess Elizabeth, 1613. Thomas Carew described him as

> a king who ruled as he thought fit
> The universal monarchy of wit,

and Ben Jonson wrote of him that he was 'the first poet in some things'.

Imperfect collections of his poems appeared in 1633–49, and 'Letters' by him in 1651. His poems were edited by Dr. Grosart in 1872–3, by C. E. Norton in 1895, by E. K. Chambers in 1896, and by H. J. C. Grierson (Oxford English Texts, 1912; Oxford Poets, 1929), the standard edition. A biography of Donne was written by Izaak Walton, published in 1640, another by E. Gosse in 1899. His name is usually pronounced and was frequently spelt 'Dunne'.

Spiller, Robert E. and others, eds. *Literary History of the United States*. New York, Macmillan, 1963. 2 vols.

The complete history is presented from colonial times to the present. Influences that shaped authors and their works are discussed in chapters written by experts. Volume II is a fine accompanying bibliography to the history. Much insight is given into the writer's works in the context of the age in which he lived. Some comments on Stephen Crane's *Red Badge of Courage* are:

"In The Red Badge of Courage Crane marks his artistic advance by moving easily from the description of the countryside, the advance and retreat of armies, the din of battle, and the color of the sky to the alternating hopes and fears of his boy soldier. . . . Crane was far in advance of the psychological knowledge of his contemporaries . . . Here is a naturalistic view of heroism unknown to the war romances of the time . . ."

And on Nathaniel Hawthorne:

"Soon after Hawthorne's birth in 1804, circumstances intensified his innate Puritan characteristics: his analysis of the mind, his somber outlook on living, his tendency to withdraw from his fellows. Yet if, from the first, in the quiet household of his widowed mother at Salem, during a period of lameness which kept him out of sports, or throughout summers in remote Raymond, Maine, he became increasingly introspective, he had few personal problems of mind or spirit."

Magill, Frank Northen. *Cyclopedia of Literary Characters*. New York, Harper & Row, 1963.

This carries brief descriptions of the principal characters of some 1,300 novels and dramas of world literature, arranged by title with a character index. Like this:

THE MEMBER OF THE WEDDING

Author: Carson McCullers (1917-   )
Time of action: 1945
First published: 1946

PRINCIPAL CHARACTERS

Frances (Frankie) Addams, a twelve-year-old girl. Jealous because she is rejected by other girls and boys in the community, she calls them names, flies into sudden rages against Berenice and John Henry, and bursts into tears of which she is ashamed. She worries over her tall, gawky frame and her big feet. She dreams romantically and excitedly of the adventures she will have with Jarvis and Janice when she accompanies them on their wedding trip, and she fights frantically when she is prevented from going. As the story ends, Frankie appears to be over the worst of her adolescence—she will be Frances from now on.

busy with his work to pay much attention to her.

Jarvis, Frankie's brother, an army corporal, a handsome blond.

Janice Evans, the fiancée of Jarvis.

Honey Camden Brown, Berenice's light-skinned, mentally weak foster brother who is jailed for robbing a store while drug-crazed.

A Soldier. He attempts to seduce Frankie but fails.

T. T. Williams, Berenice's middle-aged beau, owner of a colored restaurant.

Magill, Frank Northen. *Masterpieces of World Literature in Digest Form.* New York, Harper, 1952-1968. Vols. 1-4.

Because these volumes give plot summaries of famous books they are sometimes referred to by the original title "master-plots." Entries for each book indicate the type of work, locale, original publication date, principal characters, a very brief critique and a summary of the story. Included are such books as *Abe Lincoln in Illinois, Alice in Wonderland, Silas Marner, Seventeen* and *A Tree Grows in Brooklyn.*

Logasa, Hannah. *Historical Fiction:* guide for junior and senior high schools, and colleges, also for general reader. 8th rev. and enl. ed. Philadelphia, McKinley, 1964.

Arranged according to periods of history and places (medieval and modern Europe, Latin America, United States) this source lists and briefly annotates historical fiction. It is useful for finding works on certain historical subjects, since fiction titles alone often do not reveal the subject. A typical entry is:

1809-1868 (period covered in the story)

Allen, M. P. *Silver Fox.* McKay, 1951 (author, title, publisher)

Kit Carson and frontier life. (subject of story)

Logasa has also done the same thing for non-fiction in *Historical Non-Fiction* (Philadelphia, McKinley, 1964.)

CRITICISM

Criticism is a much maligned occupation. The word has a negative ring. Its purpose, however, is to judge and evaluate. Judgment is often favorable; evaluation is often positive. There is a false impression that criticism is easy. To a conscientious critic, it is not. The best critics will evaluate the successes and the failures of an author's entire output and compare him with writers of similar stature. Naturally, no one always agrees with critics but their opinions often lead the reader to new insights.

Book Review Digest. New York, Wilson, 1905 to date. Monthly. Annual cumulations.

Selected reviews from general magazines are given in digest form in this source. Both pro and con reviews are included, exact citations to the original review and the number of words of the original review. Main entry is by author of the book reviewed and there is a title and subject index. This sample from *Book Review Digest* is a good example of how labels can be misleading because, although the book is listed for a juvenile audience, the reader can tell by the reviews that it might also be useful to an adult student of black history:

LESTER, JULIUS. To be a slave; il. by Tom Feelings. 160p $3.95 Dial press
326 Slavery in the U.S.—Juvenile literature 26-28738

"A collection of reminiscences, experiences, and evaluations—found chiefly in narratives by ex-slaves—set down in writing both before and after the Civil War. They are . . . embedded as quotations in a . . . discussion and running commentary on the history of black Americans from the time of their abduction from Africa through their experiences on board ship, their labor on the plantations, the auction block, the futile attempts at resistance, political emancipation, the Civil War, the Ku Klux Klan, and segregation." (Horn Bk) Bibliography. "Grade nine and up." (Library J)

Reviewed by Polly Goodwin
    Book World p12 Mr 16 '69 160w
Reviewed by Donnarae MacCann
    Christian Science Monitor pB7 My 1
    '69 50w
        Horn Bk 45:65 F '69 180w

"[This is] one of the most powerful documents to appear in children's literature. . . . No library should be without this moving chronicle." M. A. Dorsey
        Library J 93:4733 D 15 '68 240w

"The author . . . trusts the capacity of the young to handle painful truths with far less

shock than they can handle hypocrisy. . . . [He makes no] degrading compromise to young readers, in the sense of diluting or bowdlerizing the texts . . . [and] ties them together in a factual, unemotional manner that throws them into brilliant relief. . . . Aside from the fact that these are tremendously moving documents in themselves, they help destroy the delusion that black men did not suffer as another man would in similar circumstances, a delusion that lies at the base of much racism today. They help also to explain the depth of the black man's current resentments. Most of them find parallels in their own present life or near past, and realize that the same fundamental myths have kept them enslaved without the actual trappings of slavery." J. H. Griffin
        N Y Times Bk R pt 2, p7 N 3 '68 600w

" 'If you want Negro history, you will have to get it from somebody who wore the shoe, and by and by from one to the other, you will get a book,' said a Tennessee slave. Julius Lester has combed through unpublished source material, extracted and organized quotations from those who wore the shoe. . . . The information is not new, but it has seldom been more effectively presented than in these carefully chosen excerpts from the bitter record of Negro history. Some of them are in dialect, some are polished, and some edited at the source; by and by, from one to the other, Lester got quite a book." Zena Sutherland
        Sat R 52:63 Mr 22 '69 110w

Moulton, Charles Wells, *Library of Literary Criticism of English and American Authors.* Buffalo, New York, Moulton Pub. Co., 1901-1905. 8 vols.

This set offers comments and criticism by and about important English and American authors. It includes brief biographical data, followed by personal views of the writer, evaluation of individual works and the general body of writing. There is an index to critics. This unusual work allows the reader to discover, for example, what Thomas Carlyle thought of Robert Burns. Robert Louis Stevenson wrote the following about Walt Whitman:

> ". . . Whitman's *Leaves of Grass,* a book of singular service, a book which tumbled the world upside down for me, blew into space a thousand cobwebs of genteel and ethical illusions . . . only a book for those who have the gift of reading."

An extension of this set into the 20th century with American authors is Dorothy Nyren's *A Library of Literary Criticism: Modern American Literature* (New York, Ungar, 1964.)

The New York Times Index

This key to articles in The Times also covers book reviews which have appeared in the daily paper and the Sunday Book Review Section. They are found under the heading "Book Reviews" and are listed by author for works by a single author and by title for all other works (anthologies, collaborations, etc.). (See chapter on Newspapers and Magazines for detailed information on the use of the *New York Times Index.*) (Note: Sources of information on authors are also described in the chapter on Biography.)

BUSINESS,
ECONOMICS
AND STATISTICS

MY own business always bores me to death; I prefer other people's." So said Oscar Wilde. Whether getting down to your own or someone else's business, there are many good reference sources.

Economic Almanac. New York, National Industrial Conference Board, 1940 to date. Biennial.

A handbook of information on business, labor and government in the United States and Canada. This almanac discusses such topics as trade, wages, standard of living and prices. A glossary of terms (agribusiness, mutual fund, yield) used in business and economics is included.

McGraw-Hill Dictionary of Modern Economics. New York, McGraw-Hill, 1965.

This dictionary of terms and organizations includes bibliographies, historical information and many tables, charts and diagrams which supplement the text. Government and private agencies are listed and nonprofit associations concerned with economics and marketing.

Coman, Edwin. *Sources of Business Information.* 2nd ed. Berkeley, Univ. of California Press, 1964.

An advanced guide, this is useful for further research. It is arranged by subject—statistics, business, finance, insurance, automation, etc. In addition to books, this work also describes periodicals such as *Survey of Current Business* and the *Federal Reserve Bulletin.*

U.S. Bureau of the Budget. *The Budget in Brief*. Washington, D.C., Government Printing Office. Annual.

The federal budget in summary form.

Business Periodicals Index. New York, Wilson, 1958 to date. Monthly except July, with annual cumulations.

A *Readers' Guide* type of guide (see Newspapers and Magazines) to magazine articles in the field of business.

Editor and Publisher Market Guide. New York, Editor and Publisher, 1924 to date. Annual.

Arranged by state and city, this book gives information under each on population, trade, banks, principal industries, etc. At right is a sample city entry; each state also has summary information and a map.

Andreane, Ralph L., Farber, Evan I., and Reynolds, Sabron. *The Student Economist's Handbook*. Cambridge, Mass., Schenkman, 1967.

A handbook which has chapters on the use of statistics, the library, and government publications. It also includes annotated lists of periodical indexes and bibliographies arranged by subject. This is a guide to business information and sources.

LIBERAL, KAN.

1—LOCATION: Seward County. E&P Map A-3 County Seat. 200 mi. SW of Wichita, Kans. on U.S. Highways 54, 83, 270.

2—TRANSPORTATION: Railroads—CRI&P. Intercity Bus Lines—Continental, Mid-Continent Coaches. Airline—Frontier.

3—POPULATION: Corp. City 60 Cen. 13,813; 70 P. Cen. 13,380 City Zone, Local Est. ....14,662 Retail Trading Zone, Local Est. ....75,338 Co. 60 Cen. 15,930; 70 Prel. Cen. 15,632 City & Retail Trading Area, Local Est. 90,000

4—HOUSEHOLDS: 60 Census, City 4,095; County ...... 4,700 Loc. Est. City 5,504; County 5,917

5—BANKS: Number   Deposits
Commercial 3 $31,356,480
Sav. & Loan Assn. .. 2 $31,716,163

6—PASSENGER AUTOS: County 7,976

7—ELECTRIC METERS: Residence 4,500

8—GAS METERS: Residence 5,000

9—PRINCIPAL INDUSTRIES (CZ): Industry. No. of Wage Earners—Grocers, Whlse. 137, Aircraft 280; RR 75; Oil & Gas 1,400; Milling 30; Truck Bed-Steel 130; Beef Packing—250; Feed Mfg.—21.

11—TAP WATER: Alkaline, medium hard. not fluoridated.

12—RETAILING: Principal Shopping Days: Mon., Wed., Sat.

13—RETAIL OUTLETS: Department Stores— C. R. Anthony Co.; J. C. Penney; Levine's; Woods. Discount Stores (CZ): Gibson's; Duckwall Alco; Surplus Outlet. Leading 5¢-$1 & Variety Stores—Woolworth; Ben Franklin. Chain Drug Stores (CZ): Johnson's Rexall. Chain Food Supermarkets: Ideal 2; Safeway; Jack & Jill. Other Chain Stores: Sweetbriar's; Mode O'Day; Grisier's; Long's; Jo-Le Shop; Casual Shop; Anna Trahern; Tucker's; Kelly's; Western Shop; Kiddie Korner; Cinderella Shop; Brown's Shoe; Oliver's Shoes; Williams Shoes; Shoeland; Montgomery Ward; Sears; Okla. Tire; Firestone; Uniroyal. Neighborhood Shopping Center—El K Cntr., 11th and Kansas Ave.; Ideal Cntr., 500 block S. Kansas Ave.

14—NEWSPAPERS: SOUTHWEST TIMES (e) 8,670 sworn Mar. 31, 1970.

Thomas' Register of American Manufacturers. New York, Thomas Publishing, 1905 to date. Annual.

This is an example of the many current directories (along with those published by Standard and Poor's and Moody's Inventment Service) available in larger reference libraries. Thomas' is several volumes arranged by product classification with an alphabetical list of manufacturers, a list of trade names, and a list by specific products. Each firm is given a symbol showing the minimum capital of the company.

STATISTICS

Pick a number, any number. Assign a meaning to it and it becomes a statistic. The world today is statistics-happy, probably because of improved and accurate methods of collecting and interpreting numerical information. In addition to the almanacs discussed in an earlier chapter and the general business sources described above, the following are outstanding statistical sources:

U.S. Bureau of the Census. *Statistical Abstract of the United States.* Washington, D.C., Government Printing Office, 1879 to date. Annual.

This single volume, issued annually, gives summary figures on the industrial, social, political and economic organization of the United States. It serves not only as a source but also as a guide to other sources since the issuing agencies are given for all tables and charts. *Statistical Abstract* deals with the current years, *Historical Statistics*, listed below, deals with the past. But today there are many more statistics gathered. The current Abstract even has figures on cultural activities (more people attend museums than symphonies) and sports and recreation (more people go bowling than play golf).

U.S. Bureau of the Census. *Historical Statistics of the United States*, colonial times to 1957, and the supplement, which is a continuation to 1962. Washington, D.C., Government Printing Office, 1960, 1965.

This source covers the same general areas as *Statistical Abstract* but in one volume it summarizes and illustrates historical periods. The reader can clearly see the trends in population, transportation, agriculture and employment. (The number of blacksmiths has been drastically reduced since 1900 and the price of sweet potatoes has risen.)

United Nations Statistical Office. *Demographic Yearbook*. New York, United Nations, 1949 to date. Annual.

A yearbook with statistics for more than 250 countries and territories on population trends, marriages, births, deaths, and life expectancy.

Statesman's Year-Book. London, New York, Macmillan, 1864 to date.

A concise guide to statistical and historical information on all countries of the world. (See note on this book in the Politics, Government and Current Events section of this guide.)

Commodity Year Book. New York, Commodity Research Bureau, 1939 to date. Annual.

Statistical data and historical information on more than 100 basic commodities—copper, cotton, gold, hogs, wheat, etc.

The Guinness Book of World Records. New York, Sterling Publishing, 1970.

An American edition of a popular British title which began as an argument settler in pubs. Information is given in quantitative terms—the tallest, the longest, the heaviest, etc. It lists such interesting trivia as the fastest talker, the longest poem, the earliest piano. The largest hailstones appeared in Potter, Nebraska, on July 6th, 1928, and were 1.5 lbs (5.4 in. diameter, 17 in. circumference!) and the stupidest creature was a stegosaurus weighing 2 tons with a brain weighing 2½ ounces.

U.S. Bureau of the Census

In addition to the *Statistical Abstract* and *Historical Statistics*, listed above, the Census Bureau publishes many reports based on the census every ten years and estimates every year. An example is the *County and City Data Book*, which has figures on counties, cities and other areas. An example of a special "subject report" put out by the Census Bureau is *Puerto Ricans in the United States;* it contains social and economic data related to persons of Puerto Rican birth and parentage. Also issued (biennially) by the Census Bureau is a paperback *Pocket Data Book USA*. This has statistical tables and factual information often given in visual forms—charts, graphs, etc. Here is a sample of the kind of information found in the very useful *Pocket Data Book*.

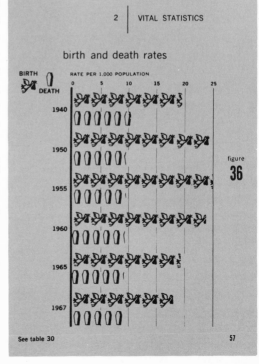

2 | VITAL STATISTICS

birth and death rates

BIRTH

DEATH

RATE PER 1,000 POPULATION

0   5   10   15   20   25

1940

1950

1955

1960

1965

1967

figure
36

See table 30

57

CUSTOMS AND HOLIDAYS

Iₙ ᴄᴀsᴇ the Latin proverb is right about custom being a tyrant, it is worth knowing why we celebrate and what habits rule us.

Hazeltine, Mary E. *Anniversaries and Holidays;* a Calendar of Days and How to Observe Them. 2nd ed. Chicago, American Library Association, 1944.

Part one of this work forms the calendar of famous feasts, holidays, and birthdays. Parts two and three give lists of books about holidays and about the people referred to in the calendar. There is a classified and general index.

Chambers, Robert. *Book of Days.* Philadelphia, Lippincott, 1899. 2 vols.

An old and charming set best described by its subtitle—"A miscellany of popular antiquities in connection with the calendar, including anecdote, biography and history, curiosities of literature, and oddities of human life and character." Under the date of January 28th, for example, there is a long, fascinating piece on "Court Fools and Jesters" which includes the following:

> "It [the custom of keeping professional fools and jesters in palaces] was founded upon, or at least was in strict accordance with, a physiological principle which may be expressed under this formula—The Utility of Laughter. Laughter is favourable to digestion, for by it the organs concerned in digestion get exercise, the exercise necessary for the process. And, accordingly, we usually find an ample meal more easily disposed of where merriment is going on, than a light one which has been taken in solitude, and under a sombre state of feeling."

It may be that this is not exactly a medically sound claim but it is an interesting one.

Walsh, William Shepard. *Curiosities of Popular Customs*. Philadelphia, Lippincott, 1898.

Walsh describes the customs of nations and discusses such items as the Blarney Stone, lampry pie at Christmas, Leap Year and May Day.

Douglas, George William. *The American Book of Days*. 2nd ed. rev. by Helen Douglas Compton. New York, H. W. Wilson, 1948.

A calendar of religious and historical celebrations which includes birthdays of famous Americans and local American festivals. The book not only tells about such days as Easter and Washington's Birthday but also discusses Cherokee Strip Day in Oklahoma, Daniel Boone Day in Kentucky and the anniversary of the Blizzard of 1888.

Chase, Harrison V. and Chase, William D. *Chases' Calendar of Annual Events*. Flint, Mich., Apple Tree Press. Annual.

This is a slender paperback calendar, issued annually, and often kept in library pamphlet files so ask for it if you don't find it in the card catalog. It includes National Library Week, Human Rights Week, and some strange local and often commercial events like Biscuit & Muffin Month, Dear Dance Day and National Mimicry Week. Here's a sample:

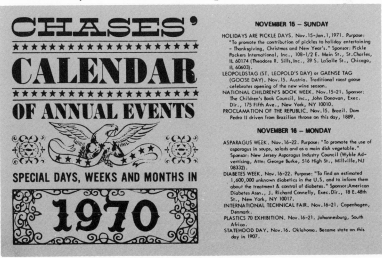

CHASES'
★ ★ ★ ★ ★ ★ ★ ★ ★ ★ ★ ★ ★ ★ ★ ★ ★ ★ ★ ★
CALENDAR
★ ★ ★ ★ ★ ★ ★ ★ ★ ★ ★ ★ ★ ★ ★ ★ ★ ★ ★ ★
OF ANNUAL EVENTS

SPECIAL DAYS, WEEKS AND MONTHS IN

1970

NOVEMBER 15 — SUNDAY

HOLIDAYS ARE PICKLE DAYS. Nov.15-Jan.1,1971. Purpose: "To promote the contribution of pickles to holiday entertaining — Thanksgiving, Christmas and New Year's." Sponsor: Pickle Packers International, Inc., 108-1/2 E. Main St., St.Charles, IL 60174 (Theodore R. Sills,Inc., 39 S. LaSalle St., Chicago, IL 60603).

LEOPOLDSTAG (ST. LEOPOLD'S DAY) or GAENSE TAG (GOOSE DAY). Nov.15. Austria. Traditional roast goose celebrates opening of the new wine season.

NATIONAL CHILDREN'S BOOK WEEK. Nov.15-21. Sponsor: The Children's Book Council, Inc., John Donovan, Exec. Dir., 175 Fifth Ave., New York, NY 10010.

PROCLAMATION OF THE REPUBLIC. Nov.15. Brazil. Dom Pedro II driven from Brazilian throne on this day, 1889.

NOVEMBER 16 — MONDAY

ASPARAGUS WEEK. Nov.16-22. Purpose: "To promote the use of asparagus in soups, salads and as a main dish vegetable." Sponsor: New Jersey Asparagus Industry Council (Wyble Advertising, Attn: George Burke, 516 High St., Millville, NJ 08332).

DIABETES WEEK. Nov.16-22. Purpose: "To find an estimated 1,600,000 unknown diabetics in the U.S. and to inform them about the treatment & control of diabetes." Sponsor:American Diabetes Assn., J. Richard Connelly, Exec.Dir., 18 E.48th St., New York, NY 10017.

INTERNATIONAL TECHNICAL FAIR. Nov.16-21. Copenhagen, Denmark.

PLASTICS 70 EXHIBITION. Nov.16-21. Johannesburg, South Africa.

STATEHOOD DAY. Nov.16. Oklahoma. Became state on this day in 1907.

EDUCATION

The MIND has been dubbed a muscle. The books below deal with how and where to exercise that muscle.

American Council on Education. *American Junior Colleges.* 7th ed. Ed. by Edmund J. Gleazer, Jr. Washington, Council, 1967.

American Council on Education. *American Universities and Colleges.* 10th ed. Ed. by Otis A. Singletary. Washington, Council, 1968.

The above two works are excellent sources of information. Arranged by state, they list colleges and universities with data on each institution's history, admission requirements, fees, degrees, staff enrollment, student aid, etc. Both also include lists of fields of study, survey articles on education and encyclopedic information on the subject.

Hawes, Gene R. *The New American Guide To Colleges.* 3rd ed. New York, Columbia University Press, 1966.

Arranged by type of institution—state colleges, liberal arts colleges for men, for women, two-year colleges, U.S., overseas, etc. There is a useful "College Discovery Index" that makes it easier to find colleges which are likely to admit, for example, a C average student, on a certain budget, in the New England

Accepts all C-aver & up admis; $300–600 exp
Broome Technical Community C, a, VI, N Y, 293
Messiah C, e, x, y, I, Pa, 101
Rutgers, The State U (U C), VII, N J, 354
St Joseph's Seraphic S, m, r, XI, N Y, 469
State U of New York Agricultural and Technical C (Alfred), VI, N Y, 296
State U Agricultural and Technical C (Delhi), e, VI, N Y, 297
State U Agricultural and Technical C (Farmingdale), VI, N Y, 297
Syracuse U (State C of Forestry), VIII, N Y, 419

area. The "College Discovery Index" is arranged by geographic region. It lists colleges according to admission policy and indicates tuition costs. (It is also published in paperback by the New American Library—complete in each college description but not inclusive of the "College Discovery Index", so finding the right one for you is not as easy.)

568   COLLEGE DISCOVERY INDEX

St Hyacinth C and S, m, r, XI, Mass,
    463

*Unclassifiable or no response admis:
    under $300 exp*
Northern Essex Community C, VI,
    Mass, 283
State C at North Adams, II, Mass,
    139
U of Connecticut, VII, Conn, 324

Other New England institutions
Auburn Maine School of Commerce,
    XII, Me, 481
Bay de Noc Community C, VI, Mass,
    283
Bay Path Junior C, w, V, Mass, 232

Silvermine C of Art, XII, Conn, 478
Simon's Rock, w, V, Mass, 234
Stevens Business C, XII, Mass, 483
Wentworth I, m, V, Mass, 234
Wheelock C, w, X, Mass, 451
Woods Hole Oceanographic Institu-
    tion, XIII, Mass, 500

2. MIDDLE ATLANTIC
(N J, N Y, Pa)

*Highly competitive admis; $1500 &
    up exp*
Albany Medical C of Union U, XIII,
    N Y, 502
Barnard C (of Columbia U), IV,
    N Y, 202

Cass, James, and Birnbaum, Max. *Comparative Guide to American Colleges for Students, Parents, and Counselors.* 1970-1971 ed. New York, Harper & Row, 1969.

An alphabetical listing of colleges with information on admission policies, campus life, costs, etc. There is a state index, a selectivity index (not a rating but an indication of the "hurdles a student will face in applying for admission") and a religious index.

Wisconsin, University of (Madison)
Wittenberg University
(+) Wooster, The College of
(+) Worcester Polytechnic Institute
Yeshiva University

Selective

Adelphi University
Akron, The University of
Alabama, University of
    College of Arts and Sciences

Very Selective (cont.)

Tulane University:
    College of Arts and Sciences
(+) Ursinus College
Valparaiso University
Vanderbilt University:
    School of Engineering
    School of Nursing
Virginia, University of:
    (+) School of Engineering and
        Applied Science
Wabash College
(+) Wake Forest University
Washington College
Washington and Jefferson College
Western Maryland College
(+) Western Reserve University
Westhampton College (University
    of Richmond)
(+) Wheaton College (Ill.)

Patterson's American Education. Mount Prospect, Ill., Educational Directories, 1904 to date. Annual.

This directory, published annually, lists public and private schools, colleges, universities and special schools in two parts: 1) School systems arranged by states and then by cities; 2) Directory of schools, colleges and universities classified by specialty. It also includes a source guide for educational materials and equipment.

Lovejoy's College Guide. Comp. by Clarence Earle Lovejoy. 11th ed. New York, Simon & Schuster, 1970.

Offers concise information on American colleges. There is a section on costs, scholarships, admissions, etc., followed by descriptions of colleges arranged by state.

Lovejoy, Clarence Earle. *Lovejoy's Career and Vocational School Guide.* 3rd ed. New York, Simon & Schuster, 1967.

Lists schools by state and also by trade in a wide variety of occupations. Job titles include nurse, beauty operator, automotive machinist, barber, baker, pilot, radio/TV repairman, sailmaker, signwriter, etc.

Lovejoy, Clarence E. *Lovejoy's Scholarship Guide.* 2nd rev. and enl. ed. New York, Simon & Schuster, 1964.

There are now many books available on this subject. Lovejoy's contains an alphabetical list of scholarships by the name of the awards and by school or college. The list will surprise you by its length and variety. There are scholarships available to war orphans, girl and boy scouts, members of minority groups, the physically handicapped, or just because you live in a certain state. There are aids available to American Indians, children of employees of certain companies and there is even one offered by the Western Golf Association whose requirement is that the "recipient must have served as a caddy with distinction at a member club of the Western Golf Association."

Feingold, S. Norman. *Scholarships, Fellowships and Loans.* Cambridge, Mass., Bellman. v. 3, 1955; v. 4, 1962
Comprehensive list arranged by administering agency with indexes by name of scholarship, fellowship or loan and by vocational goals or fields of interest. Volumes 1 and 2 are now out of print but volumes 3 and 4 effectively cover the gound in themselves.

U.S. Bureau of Labor Statistics. *Occupational Outlook Handbook.* Washington, 1949 to date. Biennial.
This handbook offers employment information on major occupations. Under occupational headings as dentists, industrial designers, bus drivers, librarians and clergy, it gives information on the nature of the work, areas where employment is to be found, training and qualifications needed, outlook, earnings and working conditions.

UNESCO. *Study Abroad;* International Handbook, fellowships, scholarships, educational exchange. Paris, United Nations Educational, Scientific and Cultural Organization, 1969.
The source deals with the possibilities of study abroad on the college and postgraduate level. The 1969 edition covers the academic years 1970-1971 and 1971-1972.

World of Learning. London, Europa Publications, 1947 to date. Annual.
World of Learning is not a guide to selecting a college. It is a reference book which, in a world list, under each country names learned societies, libraries, museums, universities, research institutes. In most instances the officers and faculties are given. There is an international section on world organizations such as UNESCO.

GEOGRAPHY

Travel cheaply, but still go first class—by book. In addition to the atlases described earlier, here are some important books about places.

The Columbia Lippincott Gazetteer of the World. Ed. by Leon E. Seltzer with the geographical staff of Columbia University Press and with the cooperation of the American Geographical Society, with Supplement. New York, Columbia University Press, 1962.

An outstanding and complete geographical dictionary listing alphabetically cities, towns, lakes, mountains, dams, canals, etc. with considerable relevant detail. It gives pronunciation, location, trade, brief history, natural resources and other pertinent facts about each place. (Note that the population figures are now out of date.) Odebolt, a town in Western Iowa, lists popcorn as its major product and calls itself the "popcorn center of the world." The gazetteer lists:

> London, England
> a London town in Arkansas
> a London city in Kentucky
> and two villages by that name.

It then goes on to describe London Bridge.

Webster's Geographical Dictionary. Rev. ed. Springfield, Mass., Merriam, 1964.

Webster's pronouncing dictionary gives brief information about the world's important places. Included are proper names from biblical times and ancient Greece and Rome to the present. The work also has many full-page and smaller inset maps.

Freeman, Otis Willard, and Morris, John, eds. *World Geography.* 2nd ed. New York, McGraw-Hill, 1965.
A good, general geography with illustrations.

Larousse Encyclopedia of World Geography. New York, Odyssey Press, 1965.
This is a well illustrated, comprehensive guide to social, economic, political and natural features of the world.

GUIDE BOOKS

Travel or guide books are an important source of geographical information whether you're planning a trip or not.

American Guide Series. Written by members of the Federal Writers Project of the Works Progress Administration. Various publishers, 1937-1950
This series covers each state and many principal cities and areas of the United States. Each book contains a section on the historical, ethnic and artistic background, a section on the cities, and a section on tours through the state. Like the Baedeker guides, this series abounds in interesting details. It is also vividly written. Here's how the article on Gettysburg from the Pennsylvania Guide begins:

"Gettysburg, scene of one of the Civil War's most decisive conflicts, lies between two low ridges eight miles north of the Mason-Dixon line. In plan it somewhat resembles a wagon wheel, with ten roads forming the spokes and its Center Square the hub . . ."

It is important with books about places to be aware of the publication dates, which may mean that certain statistics such as population are out-of-date even though the works themselves are still very useful.

Baedeker Guide Books. Leipzig, Baedeker; New York, Macmillan.

Found in larger reference centers, these are splendid volumes even though some are out of date for travel purposes. Old or new, they are extremely useful for detailed plans of cities, and minute information on buildings, streets and works of art. A 1932 guide to Paris, for example, tells how the name "Louvre" was probably derived from the word for wolfhound kennels which occupied the site at one time. It goes on to describe the Louvre's architectural development, once a castle, once a prison. The floor plans of the museum are given as well as information on the art. The Baedeker guides are filled with fascinating detail.

PLACE NAMES

Holt, Alfred H. *American Place Names.* New York, Crowell, 1938.

This is a list of place names with pronunciation amusingly given as in these examples:

> **Helena, Ala., Ark., Mont., Okla.** Stress the "hell" in these four states. But in Ohio and Missouri "lee" gets the emphasis.
>
> **La Crosse, Wis.** Just put an *l* in front of "across."
>
> **Lac Vieux Desert** (Mich. and Wis.) According to a letter from President Ellis of the Wisconsin-Michigan Lumber Company, this is "Lac Vo Desar," rhyming with "Mac, row me far." Apparently an American variation of the French-Canadian corruption. Obviously, this does not exhaust the possibilities.

Quimby, Myron J. *Scratch Ankle, U.S.A.;* American Place Names and Their Derivation. South Brunswick, N.Y., A.S. Barnes, 1969.

A discussion of, among others, Ragtown, Texas, Waterproof, La., Whiskeytown, Calif. and Scratch Ankle, Alabama.

Stewart, George R. *Names on the Land.* Rev. and enl. ed. Boston, Houghton Mifflin, 1958.

A historical account of place-naming in the United States with chapters on patterns for street names, how foreign names are used, and some chapters on individual states. There is an index.

NAMES ON THE LAND

Thus in that long period of steady development the names became more English as the strange Indian and Dutch and Swedish words were made over, but in most other ways the names became less like those of England.

Chapter XIV ❨ How they took the names into the mountains

DURING half a century, there were no new colonies; then in 1732, the fifth year of King George II, the last of the thirteen was merely called in its charter, without explanation: "The Colony of Georgia in America," thus taking the King's name with a Latin ending.

About this time the frontier began to reach the mountains. First of all went the hunters and Indian traders, but their namings often failed to be written down and preserved. Next went most often the surveyors, and the giving and recording of names came to be part of their profession. Their work was to determine the boundaries between colonies, or lay out the lines of grants. With both, they made maps, and wrote on them the names of streams and other easily recognizable features, such as outstanding or strangely shaped hills. By reference to these, other men could locate the surveyors' marks. Once thus written on a map, a name became involved with land-titles, and had a fair chance to survive.

One of the most famous surveys was that of 1728 to settle the boundary between Virginia and North Carolina, an expedition

[126]

HISTORY

Philosopher George Santayana said: "Those who cannot remember the past are condemned to repeat it." . . . condemned in the sense that the horrors of the past are repeated. So a real sense of history is a good thing and is best developed by an "in context" approach to an event. Then a student knows not only the date the Pilgrims landed in America but how they lived, what they wore, what they believed, why they came and what they found here. The books listed below are basic guides to the remembrance of the past.

WORLD HISTORY

Cambridge Ancient History. Cambridge, University Press; New York, Macmillan, 1923-39. 12 vols. 5 vols. plates, maps.

Cambridge Mediaeval History. Cambridge, University Press; New York, Macmillan, 1911-36. 8 vols.

Cambridge Modern History. Cambridge, University Press; New York, Macmillan, 1902-26. 13 vols. and atlas.

A New Cambridge Modern History. Cambridge, University Press, 1957-in progress.
This well-known series has scholarly chapters written by experts and usually includes tables and maps. The *Cambridge Modern History* has an index volume, the others are indexed in the back of each volume. (Cambridge Histories on various subjects are often confused with Oxford Companions on various subjects. Generally, the Cambridge books are done in chapter form, require the use of the index for smaller topics, and are

several volumes to a subject such as history, English literature, etc.; the Oxford Companions consist of dictionary-type entries, arranged in alphabetical order, in one volume. Examples of this difference are shown in the Books and Literature Section.)

Langer, William Leonard. *An Encyclopedia of World History.* 4th ed. rev. and enl. Boston, Houghton Mifflin, 1968.

This book is arranged chronologically—Prehistoric Period, Ancient History, Middle Ages, etc.—and within each time period it covers geographical areas—Africa, Europe, North America, etc. It is indexed and has many maps and genealogical tables. Entries are brief and bright like this sample:

> **William IV died** (1837, June 20) and was succeeded by his youthful niece, **1837-1901.   VICTORIA** (1819-1901), then eighteen.   Victoria was the daughter of the duke of Kent (d. 1820) and the duchess, a princess of Saxe-Coburg (for the Hanoverian dynasty see p. 469), who had brought up Victoria in England, but surrounded her by German influences, notably that of her brother Leopold (king of the Belgians, 1831, p. 673). Victoria's education had been solid and sensible, and she brought to her heavy duties graciousness and poise rarely associated with one of her age.   She was self-willed on occasion, "rebuked" her ministers, but made no serious attempt to invade their rights under the parliamentary system despite the influence of her German adviser, **Baron Christian von Stockmar,** who urged her to take a stand of greater independence.

Larned, Josephus Nelson. *New Larned History for Ready Reference, Reading, and Research.* Springfield, Mass., Nichols, 1922-24. 12 vols.

The approach here is unusual. It is a dictionary arrangement of universal history but it uses "the actual words of the world's best historians, biographers and specialists." Instead of original articles, under each topic recognized authorities are quoted.

The Concise Encyclopedia of Archaeology. Ed. by Leonard Cottrell. New York, Hawthorn, 1960.

The field of art might claim this work as well as the field of history (see art list for other works on archaeology). But archaeology is also a history of man, as revealed by the things he left behind. This one-volume work has an alphabetical arrangement with good, short descriptions under the headings—Athens, cave temples, Neanderthal Man, Hieroglyphs, Stonehenge, etc.

Collison, Robert, comp. *Dictionary of Dates and Anniversaries.* New York, Transatlantic Arts, 1967.

This work, with a British emphasis, has two parts. Part I is in alphabetical order by name of place, person, or event. Part II puts the same events in calendar order.

Putnam, George Palmer and Putnam, George Haven. *Dictionary of Events; a Handbook of Universal History.* New York, Grosset, 1936.

The subtitle describes the book as a "series of chronological tables presenting, in parallel columns, a record of the noteworthy events of history from the earliest times to the present day, together with an index of subjects and genealogical tables." The tabular form is useful and looks like the six columns below.

200		TABULAR VIEWS	1851 A.D.–
A.D.	PROGRESS OF SOCIETY, etc.	UNITED STATES.	GREAT BRITAIN
1851	Wyld's monster globe erected in London; employed 300 men nearly 30 days in fitting up the interior. The lord mayor of London, with several of the aldermen and common councilmen, the royal commissioners of the Exposition of Industry, etc., and the executive com-	1851. President issues a proclamation, warning all persons within the jurisdiction of the United States not to aid or engage in any expedition against the Island of Cuba, April 25. Convention of delegates from the Southern Rights Associations of South Carolina meets at	1851. The Russell Ministry resign, Feb. 22; but afterwards resume office, the Earl of Derby not having succeeded in forming a Cabinet. Hostilities with the Burmese. 1851. "The great aggregate meeting" of Roman Catholics, from all parts of the United Kingdom,

Hayes, Carlton J. H. and others. *History of Western Civilization.* New York, Macmillan, 1962.

Outline history, from the ancient Near East to the present day, covering political, military, literary and artistic events. Brief entries, illustrated and indexed.

Viorst, Milton. *The Great Documents of Western Civilization.* Philadelphia, Chilton, 1965.

Documents in history from the rise of Christianity to the Nuclear Age. Brief introductions set the scene and the text of the document follows. Includes such documents as:

Martin Luther's Ninety-Five Theses
Magna Carta
Napoleon's Proclamation at Austerlitz
Churchill's Speech after Dunkirk
United Nations Charter.

Deford, Miriam A. *Who Was When?* 2nd ed. New York, H. W. Wilson, 1952.

A dictionary of contemporaries arranged in tabular form under such headings as literature, science, government, painting. So you can see at a glance the people who made history together. You can see, for example, that Booker T. Washington, Alfred Dreyfus, and Lizzie Borden were born the same year (1859) that John Brown and Washington Irving died.

1851 A.D.	OF UNIVERSAL HISTORY		201
A.D.	FRANCE.	AUSTRIA, PRUSSIA, etc.	THE WORLD, elsewhere.
1851	Revolution: Louis Napoleon by a *coup d'etat* seizes the reins of government; dissolves the National Assembly; declares a state of siege; arrests the leaders of the opposition; constitutes an entire new ministry. The president orders the restoration of universal suffrage: an	1851. The Germanic Diet in answer to Lord Palmerston's protest against annexing the non-Germanic provinces of Austria to the Germanic Federation, says, "That no foreign interference should be allowed in a purely German question."— July 17.	1851. Hawaii:—The difficulties between the Hawaiian and French governments are arranged according to the terms of a "mutual declaration," published at Honolulu, March 25. New Granada:—Congress abolishes slavery in the republic, to take effect January 1, 1852.

Flags of the World. Rev. by E. M. C. Barraclough. New York, Warne, 1965.

Revised many times, this work now has 340 flags in color and 400 text drawings in black and white. Though there is a British emphasis, the book covers all nations.

AMERICAN HISTORY

Dictionary of American History. 2nd rev. ed. Ed. by James Truslow Adams. New York, Scribner, 1942-1961. 6 vols. and index.

Concise articles on a wide variety of subjects in American life and history. Most entries have a brief bibliography of more extensive works on the subject. "Baseball" and "Tin Pan Alley" are treated along with more serious items in U.S. history and the work includes famous slogans and popular names of laws. (See chapter on Almanacs and Atlases for information on *Atlas of American History,* also edited by Adams. This book can be used as a companion to the dictionary.)

Concise Dictionary of American History. Advisory ed., Thomas C. Cochran; ed., Wayne Andrews. New York, Scribner, 1962.

This work is a one-volume abridgment of the above-listed six-volume *Dictionary of American History.*

Kane, Joseph Nathan. *Facts About the Presidents.* 2nd ed. New York, H. W. Wilson, 1968.

A compilation of biographical and historical data in two parts. Part One has a separate chapter for each president and Part Two draws comparisons among them along such lines as elections, age when each took office, religious affiliations, etc.

Kane, Joseph Nathan. *Famous First Facts*. 3rd ed. New York, H. W. Wilson, 1964.

A book filled with curious information on such things as the first elevator, balloon, library, and even the first ice cream sundae. It is arranged alphabetically by subject and there are chronological and geographical indexes to locate events by years, days, or places.

Mirkin, Stanford M. *What Happened When*. Rev. ed. New York, I. Washburn, 1966.

A calendar of days with each event listed in chronological order by year. Emphasis is on the United States but there are some others listed. It looks like this:

JULY 18

A.D. 64   Rome burns; Nero fiddles.

1914   The U.S. Army creates an aviation section within the Signal Corps. Six airplanes are made available for aerial training.

1932   A treaty is signed between the United States and Canada for the development of the St. Lawrence River into an ocean lane and power project. (Strong opposition to the project, however, delayed actual construction until the summer of 1954.)

1938   Douglas Corrigan, who left Floyd Bennett Field, New York, on July 17 ostensibly on a flight to California, arrives at Baldonnel Airport, Dublin. (Amused Americans immediately tagged him with the nickname of "Wrong Way Corrigan.")

1940   President Franklin D. Roosevelt is nominated unanimously for a third term by delegates to the Democratic Convention at Chicago. Henry A. Wallace of Iowa is the candidate for Vice President.

1947   President Harry Truman signs the Presidential Succession Act. Under this act, when there is no Vice President, the Speaker of the House of Representatives will succeed to the Presidency, in the case of death. Next in line of succession is the president pro tempore of the Senate, followed by the members of Cabinet, beginning with the Secretary of State.

Johnson, Thomas H. *The Oxford Companion to American History*. New York, Oxford University Press, 1966.

Like the Oxford companions on other subjects, this work is a single volume of brief entries, arranged alphabetically.

Carruth, Gorton, ed. *The Encyclopedia of American Facts and Dates.* 4th ed. New York, Crowell, 1966.

This source does for American history what the Putnam's dictionary does for universal history. It is arranged chronologically in subject columns. The above illustrates how it looks.

Morris, Richard B. *The Encyclopedia of American History.* Updated and rev. New York, Harper, 1965.

Has a basic chronology of the U.S. by year, a topical chronology (under topics like "population," "laws," "religion," etc.), and a biographical section.

1909 *Pres.* THEODORE ROOSEVELT, WILLIAM H. TAFT

| POLITICS AND GOVERNMENT; WAR; DISASTERS; VITAL STATISTICS. | BOOKS; PAINTING; DRAMA; ARCHITECTURE; SCULPTURE. |

1909

National Association for the Advancement of Colored People founded to promote the rights and welfare of American Negroes.

Jan. 28 2nd military occupation of Cuba by U.S. troops ended. Last troops left island Mar. 31.

Feb. 19 Revised Homestead Act permitted entry on twice as many acres of grazing land where irrigation would not work.

Feb. 21 American battleship fleet arrived at Hampton Roads, Va., completing the round-the-world cruise. Next day the fleet was reviewed by Pres. Roosevelt.

Mar. 4 William H. Taft, 27th President, inaugurated. He was a Republican

Jack London's tempestuous life on the Pacific coast formed the basis of a semi-autobiographical novel, *Martin Eden.* Here is the story of a laborer, a seaman, who drives himself mercilessly to the heights of authorship and fame, but after overcoming all obstacles finds himself "burned out" and gives up his life to the sea.

American modern sculpture perhaps began with stay of Paul Manship at American Academy in Rome, which he left in 1912. Eschewing decorative, impressionistic and "literary" sculpture of 19th century, he put all his emphasis on design, making the details subordinate to the whole.

Savage realism represented in the painting *Both Members of This Club* by **George Bellows.** A wonderfully drawn Negro

Boatner, Mark M. *Civil War Dictionary.* New York, McKay, 1959.

Boatner, Mark M. *Encyclopedia of the American Revolution.* New York, McKay, 1966.

These two sources—each a single volume and arranged in alphabetical, dictionary form—contain information on campaigns, battles, laws and people associated with the two wars.

Commager, Henry Steele. *Documents of American History.* 7th ed. New York, Appleton, 1963. 2 vols. in 1

Beginning with the King and Queen of Spain's "privileges and prerogatives granted to Columbus," this book includes major texts in U.S. history, famous court decisions, speeches, treaties. Some of these documents make history very lively. Here is part of the "Seneca Falls declaration of sentiments and resolutions on Woman's Rights," July 19, 1848:

> The history of mankind is a history of repeated injuries and usurpations on the part of man toward woman, having in direct object the establishment of an absolute tyranny over her. To prove this, let facts be submitted to a candid world.
>
> He has never permitted her to exercise her inalienable right to the elective franchise.
>
> He has compelled her to submit to laws, in the formation of which she had no voice.
>
> He has withheld from her rights which are given to the most ignorant and degraded men—both natives and foreigners.
>
> Having deprived her of this first right of a citizen, the elective franchise, thereby leaving her without representation in the halls of legislation, he has oppressed her on all sides.
>
> He has made her, if married, in the eye of the law, civilly dead.
>
> He has taken from her all right in property, even to the wages she earns.

BLACK, AMERICAN INDIAN AND HISPANIC HISTORY

Negro Social and Political Thought 1850-1920; Representative Texts. Ed. by Howard Brotz. New York, Basic Books, 1966.

Contains the texts of famous writings by Frederic Douglass, Booker T. Washington, Marcus Garvey, etc.

Bennett, Lerone, Jr. *Before The Mayflower: A History of the Negro in America 1619-1966.* 3rd ed. Chicago, Johnson Publishing, 1966.

Chapters on black life from the "African Past" to the present time. The chapter "Landmarks & Milestones" is a chronology of events and people.

Franklin, John Hope. *From Slavery to Freedom; A History of Negro Americans.* 3rd ed. New York, Knopf, 1967.

Frazier, E. Franklin. *The Negro in the United States.* Rev. ed. New York, Macmillan, 1957.

Hughes, Langston, and Meltzer, Milton. *Pictorial History of the Negro in America.* New York, Crown, 1968.

Woodson, Carter G., and Wesley, Charles H. *The Negro in Our History.* 10th ed. Washington, D.C., Associated Publishers, 1962.
    Four general histories of the Negro.

Forbes, Jack D. *The Indian in America's Past.* Englewood Cliffs, N.J., Prentice-Hall, 1964.
    An understanding look at Indian heritage beginning with a chapter "When Worlds Collide" that describes the encounter between native Americans and the first European arrivals. There are chapters on "Red Slavery," U.S. policy toward the Indians and an extremely useful chapter, "Voices From Native America," which contains Indian narratives and speeches.

Josephy, Alvin M., Jr. *The Indian Heritage of America.* New York, Alfred A. Knopf, 1968.
    This book begins by making the important distinction between stereotypes and the "Real Indian." There are chapters on various tribes in different parts of America and the work concludes with a chapter on "Indians Today and Their Fight For Survival," for indeed their struggle continues.

97

American Heritage Book of Indians. Ed. in Charge, Alvin M. Josephy, Jr., and narrative by William Brandon. New York, American Heritage, 1961.
An excellent source, in chapter form but with an index, and beautifully illustrated.

Hodge, Frederick Webb. *Handbook of American Indians North of Mexico.* Washington, Government Printing Office, 1907-1910. (Repr.: New York, Pageant Books, 1959) 2 vols.
Dictionary entries, some quite long, on all phases of Indian life (education, games, food, etc.), on tribes such as the Sioux and the Cherokee, and on famous people like Crazy Horse and Sitting Bull.

Swanton, John R. *The Indian Tribes of North America.* Washington, Government Printing Office, 1952.
A source arranged by state and under each state a list of tribes with the origin of the name, location and brief history.

Steiner, Stan. *The New Indians.* New York, Harper & Row, 1968.
Contemporary history of the New Indian who seeks to maintain his unique cultural heritage through Red Power and the end of "Uncle Tomahawk."

Again, the standard reference books are listed here, but remember to check the card catalog of your library for current, unusual, or more specific subjects and treatment. You might find, for example:

McWilliams, Carey. *North From Mexico; The Spanish-Speaking People of the United States.* Philadelphia, Lippincott, 1949. (Repr.: New York, Greenwood Press, 1968)

Senior, Clarence. *The Puerto Ricans; Strangers—Then Neighbors.* Chicago, published in cooperation with the Defamation League of B'nai B'rith by Quadrangle Books, 1965.

Wakefield, Dan. *Island in the City; Puerto Ricans in New York.* New York, Corinth Books, 1957.

GUIDES TO HISTORY

Finally, for advanced research in a field as important as history, the following titles are guides to the literature and study of history. The first title is for general history, the second is for American history and the third title is an excellent research methods and reference guide which is of particular help in the evaluation and interpretation of facts and the study of history.

American Historical Association. *Guide to Historical Literature.* Ed. by George Frederick Howe and others. New York, Macmillan, 1961.

Handlin, Oscar, and others. *Harvard Guide to American History.* Boston, Harvard University Press, 1954. (Atheneum, 1967)

Barzun, Jacques, and Graff, Henry F. *The Modern Researcher.* New York, Harcourt, Brace & World, 1957.

INDUSTRIAL ARTS

Aₙʏₒₙₑ who has tried to develop a manual skill knows why the activity is called an art.

Boumphrey, Geoffrey. *Engines and How They Work.* Rev. ed. New York, Franklin Watts, 1967.

Boumphrey's aim is to make the "most complex engine readily intelligible to the most unmechanically minded layman." The study ranges from the simplicity of the primitive steam engine designed by Hero of Alexandria in the first century to the complexities of the modern turbojet.

Motor's Auto Repair Manual. New York, Motor, 1970. Annual.

Everything on how to repair a car is here including how to push and tow cars. A troubleshooting section has an index of symptoms covering parts from transmissions to brakes and windshield wipers. There is also an index by make of car and Motor's is well illustrated.

Chilton's Auto Repair Manual. Philadelphia, Chilton, 1970. Annual.

Another standard, illustrated repair manual. Until 1967 this was called *Glenn's Auto Repair Manual.*

Glenn, Harold T. *Glenn's Foreign Car Repair Manual.* 2nd ed. Philadelphia, Chilton, 1966.

An illustrated work like the above but dealing with foreign cars.

Clymer, Floyd. *A Treasury of Motorcycles of the World.* New York, McGraw-Hill, 1965.

A complete guide to the history and technique of motorcycling. It includes chapters with illustrations on the art of riding, competitions and shows, and information about engines and new developments. There is also a touring and camping guide.

Petersen, Robert E. *Complete Book of Hot Rodding.* Englewood Cliffs, New Jersey, Prentice-Hall, 1959.
As the title suggests, it is a complete guide to the sport and it has a "hot rod glossary." Compiled by Petersen and the editors of Hot Rod Magazine.

American Radio Relay League. *The Radio Amateur's Handbook.* Newington, Conn., American Radio Relay League, 1970, Revised annually.
This handbook is written with the needs of the practical amateur in mind. It treats radio communications problems in terms of how-to-do-it rather than abstract discussion. Chapters on electrical laws and circuits, receiving systems, code transmission, wave propagation, assembling a station, etc. The book contains many diagrams, charts and photographs.

Hahn, Steven. *Hi-fi Handbook:* a guide to monaural and stereophonic reproduction, 2nd ed. rev. by William Kendall. New York, Thomas Y. Crowell, 1962.
Information, much of it nontechnical, on understanding, evaluating and installing high-fidelity equipment.

The above list merely suggests what is available in the field. Check the subject headings of your library catalog for other titles. There is also a good series published by Audel (Indianapolis) with titles beginning with "Audels Practical Guide to . . ." covering subjects like tape recorders, electricity, electronics, technical trades, etc. The authors vary but the titles begin with "Audels . . ."

MATHEMATICS

There was a young fellow from Trinity
Who took $\sqrt{\infty}$
But the number of digits
Gave him the fidgets.
He dropped math and took up divinity.

FROM: *One, Two Three . . . Infinity*
(see books on Science)

MATHEMATICS developed from a primeval need. Man wanted to know things like the number of animals in his flocks and had an impulse to keep track of the passage of time, which most likely led him to record the changing face of the heavens. The library will have individual books on arithmetic, algebra, geometry, etc. Count on those listed here for general information on all aspects of math.

The World of Mathematics. Ed. by James R. Newman. New York, Simon & Schuster, 1956. 4 vols.

This is a small library of the famous literature of mathematics from A'h-mosé the Scribe to Albert Einstein. It includes discussions of all aspects of math, ranging from mathematical ways of thinking to the laws of probability and chance. These four volumes convey "the diversity, the utility and the beauty of mathematics." The historical and biographical material will be useful to all but some of the literature included is of use only to those with special interest in the subject. There is an article, for example, by Archimedes, whose fascination with large numbers is revealed in his "cattle problem" solution. This consisted of eight numbers which, when written out, would require almost 700 pages. The material is fascinating but this is not a set for someone boning up on his math.

Universal Encyclopedia of Mathematics. Foreword by James R. Newman. New York, Simon & Schuster, 1964.

A compact one-volume work which, in Part 1, has articles arranged alphabetically by subject; Part 2 contains mathematical formulas; Part 3, mathematical tables. Covers mathematics from arithmetic through calculus.

Hogben, Lancelot. *Mathematics for the Million.* 4th rev. ed. New York, Norton, 1968.

The lore and theory of mathematics are here, including such aspects as mathematics for the mariner. There are those who will think it appropriate that an article on how algebra began is titled "The Dawn of Nothing." Shown on this and the following page are illustrations from Hogben's book that deal with the early history of math.

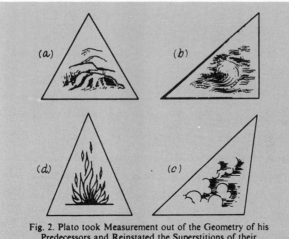

Fig. 2. Plato took Measurement out of the Geometry of his Predecessors and Reinstated the Superstitions of their Ancestors

The real world of Plato was a world of form from which matter was banished.

(a) An *equilateral* triangle (i.e. one of which all three sides are equal) is the elemental earth form.

(b) A *right-angled* triangle is the spirit of water. (To find spirit in water is the most advanced kind of magic.)

(c) A *scalene* triangle with no equal sides is the spirit of the air.

(d) An *isosceles* triangle (i.e. one of which only two sides are equal) is the elemental fire.

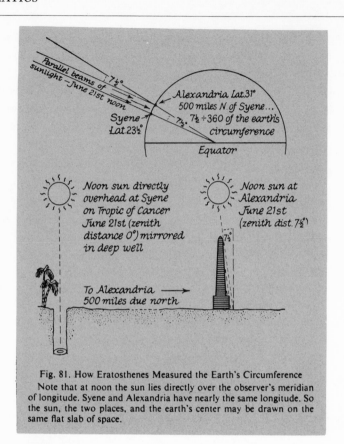

Fig. 81. How Eratosthenes Measured the Earth's Circumference

Note that at noon the sun lies directly over the observer's meridian of longitude. Syene and Alexandria have nearly the same longitude. So the sun, the two places, and the earth's center may be drawn on the same flat slab of space.

James, Glenn, and James, Robert C. *Mathematics Dictionary.* (Multilingual) 3rd ed. New York, Van Nostrand-Reinhold, 1968.

Definitions range from terms in high school geometry and algebra to more advanced university topics. It is designed to meet the needs of both students and scholars.

Turnbull, Herbert Westren. *The Great Mathematicians.* New York, New York University Press, 1961.

These brief biographies of men like Descartes and Isaac Newton reveal the history of math through interesting lives.

Naft, Stephen. *International Conversion Tables.* Expanded and rev. by Ralph DeSola. New York, Duell, Sloan and Pearce, 1961.

An accurate ready-reference for converting U.S. weights, measures, currencies, etc., into foreign equivalents. See example below in case you ever need a quart of milk in Russia.

CAPACITÉ (LIQUIDES)	CAPACITY (Liquids)		CAPACIDAD (LIQUIDOS)
AMERICAN (U. S. and CANADA)		METRIC	RUSSIAN
Units	Subdivisions		
1 Cubic Foot	7.4805 U. S. gallon 6.229 British gallon	28.317 liters	2.3024 vedros 23.0242 shtoffs
1 U. S. Gallon (gal.)	0.13368 cubic feet 231 cubic inches 0.83259 British gallon 4 U. S. quarts 8 U. S. pints 32 U. S. gills 128 U. S. fluid ounces 1024 U. S. fluid drams 3.33036 British quarts 8.3356 lbs. of water	0.03785 hectoliters 3.78533 liters	0.3078 vedro 3.0781 shtoffs
1 U. S. Quart (qt.)	0.25 U. S. gallon 2 U. S. pints 8 U. S. gills 32 U. S. fluid ounces 256 U. S. fluid drams 0.83259 British quart 0.20817 British gallon	0.946333 liter	0.07695 vedro 0.7695 shtoff
1 U. S. Pint (pt.)	4 U. S. gills 16 U. S. fluid ounces 128 U. S. fluid drams 0.83259 British pint	0.473167 liter	0.3847 shtoffs 3.847 charkas
1 U. S. Gill (gi.)	1920 U. S. minims 32 U. S. fluid drams 4 U.S. fluid ounces 0.83259 British gill	0.118292 liter	0.0962 shtoff
1 U. S. Fluid Ounce (fl. oz.)	1.0407 British fluid ounces 0.0078125 U. S. gallon	2.9573 centiliters 29.573 cubic centimeters	0.02405 shtoff 0.2405 charkas

From the book: INTERNATIONAL CONVERSION TABLES by Ralph DeSola.

Zimmerman, Oswald Theodore, and Lavine, Irvin. *Industrial Research Service's Conversion Factors and Tables.* 3rd ed. Dover, N.H., Industrial Research Service, 1961.

Another excellent book of conversion tables.

MUSIC

Hᴇᴀʀ with your eyes. That's the opportunity offered by some books on the subject of music.

Grove, Sir George. *Dictionary of Music and Musicians*. 5th ed. Ed by Eric Blom. New York, St. Martin's Press, 1954. 9 vols. and supplement 1961.

This standard work covers the whole field of music from 1450 on and includes musical and related terms such as "Buffo" and subjects like the Berkshire festivals, music history, theory and practice and musical instruments. Bibliographies are given and the complete catalogues of works of major musicians. Biographies are comprehensive for major figures such as Wagner and brief for obscure people such as Wynkyn de Worde, an Alsatian printer who was the first to print music in London. Grove's is illustrated with photographs and drawings.

Scholes, Percy A. *The Concise Oxford Dictionary of Music*. 2nd ed. New York, Oxford University Press, 1964.

An illustrated dictionary giving brief information on composers, musical compositions, performances, and terminology.

Kobbé, Gustave. *Kobbé's Complete Opera Book*. Ed. and rev. by Lord Harewood. New York, G. P. Putnam, 1963.

W. H. Auden once said that no good opera plot can be sensible, for people do not sing when they are feeling sensible. Sensible or not, Kobbé's is the place to go for plot summaries and general information. Music for the important motifs is usually given. The period covered includes modern times, concluding with Menotti and George Gershwin's "Porgy and Bess."

Lubbock, Mark H. *Complete Book of Light Opera*. Des Moines, Iowa, Appleton-Century-Crofts, 1963.

Intended as a companion to Kobbé's opera book, this source covers light opera in Paris, Vienna, Berlin and London from 1850 to 1961. There is an American section by David Ewen which includes works like "Cabin in the Sky" and "The Sound of Music." Musical themes are given along with plot—as shown in this example, the conclusion to a description of the 1903 London production of "A Princess of Kensington:"

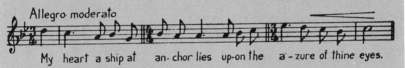

Having settled her own love affair happily, Kenna asks Puck to straighten out the situation between poor Brook Green and Joy. Brook Green has come to Winklemouth, disguised as a boatman, to find Joy. Here he sings of his longing for her:

Allegro moderato

My heart a ship at an-chor lies up-on the a - zure of thine eyes.

But although Joy is pleased to see Brook, she teases him and they have a quarrel. In despair Brook finds the Recruiting Sergeant and joins the Marines. Joy is dreadfully upset when she hears this, but when Sir James Jellicoe himself appears he rectifies matters by explaining that Brook Green is in his employ and may not enlist without his permission. So Joy's lover is restored to her. Nell decides to marry Uncle Ben and that is the happy end to the Midsummer Day.

From the book COMPLETE BOOK OF LIGHT OPERA by Mark H. Lubbock.

Light opera may be dead.

Fuld, James J. *Book of World-Famous Music;* classical, popular, and folk. New York, Crown, 1966.

Data on thousands of songs, tunes, etc. They are alphabetically indexed with musical theme, words, date of first appearance and brief biographical information on composers and lyricists.

Shapiro, Nat. *Popular Music, An Annotated Index of American Popular Songs.* New York, Adrian Press, 1964-1966. 3 vols.

Listing popular songs published 1940 to 1964, this index is arranged by year and then by title. It gives author, title, composer, publisher, and first or best selling record with performer and record company.

Baker, Theodore. *Baker's Biographical Dictionary of Musicians.* 5th ed. Completely revised by Nicolas Slonimsky. New York, Schirmer, 1958, with supplement, 1965.

This reliable dictionary compactly gives biographies of musicians of all ages and nations. Informative and useful, it reveals, for example, that Irving Berlin received no formal music training and never learned to read or write music, and the anguish of Beethoven who, in the isolation of his deafness, created some of the world's great music.

Sears, Minnie Earl. *Song Index.* New York, Wilson, 1926, and supplement 1934. Hamden, Conn., Shoe String Press, 1966. 2 vols. in 1.

The Song Index gives references to thousands of songs which may be found in over 150 collections. It contains titles, first lines, authors' names and composers' names in one alphabet. Useful for locating the music and words of a song and lists of songs by an author or composer.

Thompson, Oscar. *International Cyclopedia of Music and Musicians.* 9th ed. Ed. by Robert Sabin. New York, Dodd, 1964.

Here is an excellent one-volume encyclopedia on music. It covers a wide range of topics from the Braille system to Negro music to music criticism.

Lawless, Ray M. *Folksingers and Folksongs in America*. 2nd ed. New York, Duell, 1965.

This guide to folk music includes biographies and an anotated bibliography of collections of folk songs. It is illustrated with paintings by Thomas Hart Benton and photographs such as one which shows the log cabin where "Home on the Range" was written in 1873. It even takes on the definition of a folk song:

"But a folksong is not easily defined. A ballad is a folksong, but a folksong is not a ballad unless it tells a story . . . the Shanty . . . is a folksong. A spiritual is a religious folksong. The blues, a predominantly melancholy type of jazz may be a folksong . . . But the specific characteristics of a general, traditional folksong . . . are these: it is music that has been submitted to the process of oral transmission; it is the product of evolution and is dependent on the circumstances of continuity, variation, and selection."

Feather, Leonard. *The Encyclopedia of Jazz*. Rev. ed. New York, Horizon Press, 1960.

In the introduction to this work, Benny Goodman says that he believes jazz is one of our most original contributions to Twentieth Century culture and seems likely to go down in history as the real folk music of our country. The Encyclopedia is primarily made up of biographies of famous jazz musicians (Dave Brubeck, Ella Fitzgerald, Charles Mingus) but it also has a historical survey, a chronology of jazz, and related articles. Bringing the subject up to date and adding new material is this same author's *The Encyclopedia of Jazz in The Sixties* (New York, Horizon Press, 1966).

The Dance Encyclopedia. Rev. ed. Ed. by Anatole Chujoy and P. W. Manchester. New York, Simon & Schuster, 1967.

A guide which has long, signed articles as well as brief references to many subjects connected with dance. Includes information on various ballet companies, biographies, material on national dances (American, Oriental, Soviet, etc.).

Ewen, David. *The Complete Book of the American Musical Theater.* New York, Holt, 1958.

A subtitle describes this as a guide to more than 300 productions of the American musical theater, listing stars, songs, composers, etc. and giving the plots. This same author, David Ewen, has edited several other books about music and musicians which vary in usefulness.

Garland, Phyl. *The Sound of Soul.* Chicago, Henry Regnery, 1969.

Cohn, Nik. *Rock From The Beginning.* New York, Stein and Day, 1969.

Malone, Bill C. *Country Music U.S.A.: A Fifty Year History.* Austin, University of Texas Press, 1968.

These titles are given as examples of the kind of current material on music which can be found under the subject heading in the library card catalog. Though not "standard" reference sources they are indexed and include up-to-date information on contemporary music.

MYTHOLOGY

MYTHS are entertaining and, as the science, religion and literature of primitive people, they are important. Beyond that, think how deprived our language should be without the elegance and instant recognition of stories and names like Pandora, Cupid, and the Lotus Eaters.

Mythology of All Races. Boston, Marshall Jones, 1916-1932. 13 vols.

A leading reference work in the field, this set is arranged by race and has a general index. It discusses myths surrounding thunder, fire and wind, etc., in the view of various races.

Gayley, Charles Mills. *The Classic Myths.* Boston, Ginn, 1911.

This is a one-volume work which treats classical myths in relation to English literature and art. Based originally on Bulfinch's *Age of Fable*, it includes chapters on Norse and German myths. It is filled with notes like the one that Venus, goddess of love and beauty, was called Aphrodite by the Greeks because the word means "foam-born" and they believed she arose from the foam of the sea. It then places her in literature and art (the "Venus de Milo," for example).

Frazer, Sir James G. *New Golden Bough;* a new abridgment of the classic work. Ed. by Theodor H. Gaster. New York, S. G. Phillips, 1959.

Description and interpretation of beliefs and customs related to magic and religion. This is an abridgment of the comprehensive original 12 volume set.

Bulfinch, Thomas. *Bulfinch's Mythology:* The Age of Fable; The Age of Chivalry; Legends of Charlemagne. Rev. ed. New York, Crowell, 1962.

Bulfinch's presents the stories of King Arthur and Charlemagne as well as Greek and Roman myths. A "dictionary index" (sample below) is useful for quickly identifying references from mythology.

Gor'gons, three monstrous females, with huge teeth, brazen claws and snakes for hair, sight of whom turned beholders to stone; Medusa, the most famous, slain by Perseus (which *See*), 115.

Gor'lois, Duke of Tintadel, 397, 398.

Gou-ver-nail, squire of Isabella, queen of Lioness, protector of her son Tristram while young, 449, and his squire in knighthood, 463.

Graal, the Holy, cup from which the Saviour drank at Last Supper, taken by Joseph of Arimathea to Europe, and lost, its recovery becoming a sacred quest for Arthur's knights, 392, 475, 487.

Graces, three goddesses who enhanced the enjoyments of life by refinement and gentleness; they were Aglaia (brilliance), Euphrosyne (joy), and Thalia (bloom), 4, 8.

Gra-das'so, king of Sericane, 672, 700, 702, 737, 740, 765, 768-769, 784-788.

Græ'æ, three gray-haired female watchers for the Gorgons, with one movable eye and one tooth between the three, 115-116.

Grimal, Pierre, ed. *Larousse World Mythology.* Tr. by Patricia Beardsworth. New York, G. P. Putnam's Sons, 1965.

This handsomely illustrated book presents chapters on the mythologies of geographical regions throughout the world. They are all here—god Gou of Dahomey and the magic animals of the Uralian peoples, for example. The Larousse is a work which will be of interest to the art and literature student because of its emphasis on "myths which have been important in the life and literature of man from prehistoric times to the present."

PARLIAMENTARY PROCEDURE

T HERE is no escaping it. Books on "rules of order" seem to lack order. Well, the rules are listed in an orderly way but the language is unruly. The standard works are based on the rules and practice of Congress (a body not noted for its orderly behavior) and, though they have been revised and simplified, they are still essentially what they were in 1876. Try reading the section on "Quasi Committee of the Whole (Consideration as if in Committee of the Whole)" or the instructions on "Creating a Blank." And if you think you're tired now, read the following on the "Exhaustion of the Previous Question."

> **EXHAUSTION OF THE PREVIOUS QUESTION.** The *Previous Question* is said to be *exhausted* (in reference to a particular order for it) when all of the motions on which it was ordered have been finally disposed of, or when any motions not yet finally disposed of are no longer affected by the order. The conditions for exhaustion of the *Previous Question* are the same as for an order limiting or extending limits of debate—that is: (1) when all motions on which the *Previous Question* was ordered have been voted on; (2) when those not yet voted on have either been committed or postponed indefinitely; or (3) at the end of the session in which the *Previous Question* was ordered—whichever occurs first. After the *Previous Question* is exhausted, any remaining questions that come up again are open to debate and amendment just as if there had been no order for the *Previous Question*.

Of course, it's not quite fair out of context and, alas, no meeting can function without guidelines. The newly revised edition of the standard reference, *Robert's Rules of Order*, is a great improvement and the best book on the subject.

Robert, Henry M. *Robert's Rules of Order*. Newly rev. ed. by Sarah Corbin Robert and others. Glenview, Ill., Scott, Foresman, 1970.

PHILOSOPHY AND RELIGION

Beliefs, life styles and views of the universe are the topics in these sources.

The Concise Encyclopedia of Western Philosophy and Philosophers. Ed. by J. O. Urmson, New York, Hawthorn Books, 1960.

These brief articles, written by British scholars, cover biographical material, major philosophies, and define terms like "determinism" and "existentialism." As indicated in the title only "Western" philosophy is covered.

Masterpieces of World Philosophy in Summary Form. Ed. by Frank N. Magill. New York, Harper, 1961.

This book includes brief summaries of all major philosophies and religions, both Eastern and Western. It ranges from Plato to Martin Buber, to Confucius, St. Augustine and Jean-Paul Sartre. Each summary begins with a short description of the "principal ideas advanced" and then elaborates.

I AND THOU

Author: Martin Buber (1878-   )
Type of work: Theology, epistemology
First published: 1923

PRINCIPAL IDEAS ADVANCED

There is no independent "I" but only the I existing and known in objective relation to something other than itself, an "It," or as encountered by and encompassed by the other, the "Thou."

Just as music can be studied analytically by reference to its notes, verses, and bars, or encountered and experienced in such a manner that it is known not by its parts but as a unity, so the I can relate itself analytically to something other, "It," or it can encounter the other, "Thou," so as to form a living unity.

The "Thou" stands as judge over the "It," but as a judge with the form and creative power for the transformation of "It."

Each encountered "Thou" reveals the nature of all reality, but finally the living center of every "Thou" is seen to be the eternal "Thou."

The eternal "Thou" is never known objectively, but certitude comes through the domain of action.

Gaer, Joseph. *What the Great Religions Believe*. New York, Dodd Mead, 1963.

Gaer's work describes Eastern religions as well as Judaism and Christianity. Kipling may have been wrong about "East is East, and West is West, and never the twain shall meet." Today there seems to be a lot of interest, for example, in Zen, which this book describes this way:

"To comprehend Zen one must first discipline and restrain the mind through meditation and introspection, without the use of logical thinking, avoiding the pitfalls of verbalization. The ultimate aim is to obtain an entirely new view of all experience. And the key word is Satori (enlightenment) . . . Zen encourages search *into* rather than *outside* oneself for enlightenment. If the question is properly 'felt' the answer is instantly received."

Encyclopedia of Philosophy. Ed. by Paul Edwards. New York, Macmillan, 1967. 8 vols.

A very scholarly set found in larger library collections. It covers both Oriental and Western concepts and philosophers for all periods. Articles are signed and followed by bibliographies.

Gibb, H. A. R., and Kramer, J. H., eds. *Shorter Encyclopedia of Islam*. Ithaca, N.Y., Cornell University Press, 1953.

All aspects of the Islamic religion are included—people, customs, places, laws.

Mead, Frank S. *Handbook of Denominations in the United States*. 5th ed. Nashville, Tenn., Abingdon Press, 1970.

Factual and historical information arranged by denomination and giving basic beliefs of each. It also indicates different groups within a major denomination.

Yearbook of American Churches. New York, National Council of Churches of Christ in the U.S.A., 1916 to date. Annual.

Directory and statistical information on all faiths. Includes religious agencies and organizations. (In addition, there are put out by individual religions such as the *American Jewish Yearbook* and the *National Catholic Almanac.*)

Hastings, James. *Dictionary of the Bible.* Rev. ed. by Frederick C. Grant and H. H. Rowley. New York, Scribner, 1963.

Contains maps and chronologies in addition to the dictionary entries under headings such as "Dreams" and "Good Samaritan." Cites exact references to chapter and verse in the Bible where story or subject appears. It is both specific and detailed. For example, under "Ant" it points out that ants are mentioned only twice in the Bible and then cites the instances.

There are all kinds of aids to Bible study—atlases, concordances, and Bible quotation books. Examples are:

May, Herbert G. and others. *Oxford Bible Atlas.* New York, Oxford University Press, 1962.

Stevenson, Burton E. *Home Book of Bible Quotations.* New York, Harper & Row, 1949.

Cruden, Alexander. *Cruden's Unabridged Concordance to the Old and New Testaments and the Apocrypha.* Grand Rapids, Mich., Baker Book House, 1953.

New Catholic Encyclopedia. Prep. by an editorial staff at the Catholic University of America. New York, McGraw-Hill, 1967. 15 vols.

The *New Catholic Encyclopedia* and the two encyclopedias listed below are broad enough for general use as well as religious reference. The fine *New Catholic Encyclopedia* has scholarly and readable articles, signed and with select bibliographies. In line with today's ecumenical trends some of the articles are written by non-Catholics, such as the one on Christian Science, written by E. D. Canham, editor of the *Christian Science Monitor.* The encyclopedia covers doctrine, religious institutions, philosophies and scientific and cultural developments affecting the Catholic Church from its beginning to the present.

Jewish Encyclopedia. New York, Funk & Wagnalls, 1901-6. 12 vols.

"A descriptive record of the history, religion, literature, and customs of the Jewish people from the earliest times to the present day." Though old, this scholarly set is very useful for its biographies and historical information. The brief article on "Apple" is an example of its unique and learned approach. The apple is discussed in terms of Biblical data, in terms of its symbolic meaning in Rabbinical literature, and from a botanical point of view. And there is a separate, shorter article on the Apple of Sodom, or Dead Sea Apple, which was "externally of fair appearance, but turning to smoke and ashes when plucked with the hands."

Roth, Cecil, ed. *The Standard Jewish Encyclopedia.* New rev. ed. Garden City, N.Y., Doubleday, 1966.

Presents historical events and all phases of Jewish life in one volume. More up to date than the encyclopedia listed above and it emphasizes American subjects and life.

PLAYS

"DRAMA—what literature does at night." So said critic George Jean Nathan. When the play's your thing, some things to consult are:

Shipley, Joseph Twadell. *Guide to Great Plays.* Wash., Public Affairs Press, 1956.

The guide lists by author great plays of all times. It gives a digest of each play in addition to information on famous productions, casts and reviews.

Hartnoll, Phyllis. *Oxford Companion to the Theatre.* 3rd ed. London, New York, Oxford University Press, 1967.

Like other Oxford Companions, this is a one-volume work arranged in dictionary form. It is international in scope and includes such things as articles on Jewish theatre, on make-up and lighting and on individuals such as Russian dramatist Anton Chekhov and Negro Shakespearean actor Ira Aldridge.

Campbell, Oscar James, and Quinn, Edward G., eds. *The Reader's Encyclopedia of Shakespeare.* New York, Thomas Y. Crowell, 1966.

An excellent one volume source of information on Shakespeare. Arranged in dictionary form, it discusses actors, characters, adapters, etc. For each play it considers sources, plots, stage history (productions), and selected criticism. The smallest details are given. Even "Crab," the dog in *The Two Gentlemen From Verona,* is given an entry.

Biographical Encyclopedia and Who's Who in the American Theatre. Ed. by Walter Rigdon. New York, James H. Heineman, 1966.

An informative work containing biographical information on contemporary actors, producers, directors, etc. It also has a list of productions with opening dates, number of performances, and lists of awards. In addition to information about people, the book has a list of "theatre building biographies." Here is a sample:

OLYMPIA, east side of Broadway between 44th and 45th Sts. Owner, Oscar Hammerstein. Architect, J. B. McElfatrick and Son. The complex consisted of a music hall, a concert hall, a theatre, a roof garden, etc. Opening of what was called the LYRIC THEATRE, November 25, 1895, with *Excelsior, Jr.* The MUSIC HALL, opened with Yvette Guilbert, December 17, 1895.
MUSIC HALL re-opened as:
NEW YORK THEATRE, April 24, 1899, with *The Man in the Moon*
LYRIC THEATRE, reopened as:
CRITERION THEATRE, August 29, 1899, with *The Girl from Maxim's*
VITAGRAPH THEATRE, February 7, 1914, as a cinema theatre
CRITERION THEATRE, September 11, 1916, with *Paganini*
Demolished 1935

PALLADIUM, 254 W. 54th St., between Broadway and 8th Ave.
(See GALLO THEATRE)

Gassner, John, and Quinn, Edward G., eds. *The Reader's Encyclopedia of World Drama.* New York, Thomas Y. Crowell, 1969.

A one-volume book with emphasis on drama as literature. It has information on plays and playwrights from all countries and has an appendix containing "basic documents in dramatic theory."

In large libraries indexes to plays in collections and full texts of plays are available as well as "best plays" series. And *The New York Times Index*, under the heading "Theatre Reviews," will lead you to the opinions of the Times critics.

POETRY

THERE IS an ugly rumor that nobody reads poetry any more but still it continues to be written and quoted. Certainly poetry is elusive and probably was best described by poet Maxwell Bodenheim, who called it the impish attempt to paint the color of the wind.

Granger's Index to Poetry. 5th ed. Ed. by William F. Bernhardt. New York, Columbia University Press, 1962. Supplement, 1967.

This is the most complete index to individual poems in collections of poetry. It has three indexes: one by author (where you will find under the author's name a useful alphabetical list of his poems), a subject index and a title and first line index. The title index is the main entry and looks like this:

> Schoolroom on a Wet Afternoon. Vernon Scannell.
> HaMU.

"Schoolroom . . ." is the title, Scannell is the author, and HaMU is the symbol for a collection of poetry in which the poem will be found. In this case the symbol stands for *The Harrap Book of Modern Verse.* (A key to the symbols is located in the front of Granger's.) This poem is also indexed under its first line, by author and in the subject index under "schoolroom."

Preminger, Alexander, ed. *Encyclopedia of Poetry and Poetics.* Princeton University Press, 1965.

A lively book with signed articles usually accompanied by bibliographies. The work includes articles you would expect to find like those on rhyme and meter but also some unusual ones—for example, "The Fleshly School of Poetry"—and here's how the one on "Poetic Madness" begins:

POETIC MADNESS. In *Phaedrus 245* Socrates asserts that poets are susceptible to madness and, in fact, cannot succeed without it. In the *Ion* both poet and critic are described as possessed by a frenzy so that they do not consciously control their words. In Aristotle's *Problemata 30* it is said that poets and philosophers are inclined to excessive melancholy. Roman poets are possessed by spirits or demons (Ovid: "Deus est in nobis/Agitante calescimus illo"—"A god is within us; when he urges, we are inspired"); write best when tipsy (Horace); are filled with the divine afflatus (Cicero); or are literally mad (the tradition that Lucretius was driven insane by a love potion). The concept of p.m., which can be found *passim* in European poetry and criticism, is summed up in two familiar quotations: "The lunatic, the lover, and the poet/Are of imagination all compact" (Shakespeare); and "Great wits are sure to madness near allied/And thin partitions do their bounds divide" (Dryden).

The parallel between poets and madmen is extremely primitive. It apparently goes back to the time when the poet, the prophet, and

It is well cross referenced, too. Under a brief article on "Haiku" (3-line poems which must state or imply a season and use natural images) there is a see reference to a long article on "Japanese Poetry" which has a few examples of Haiku. Here is one:

The moon passes
In splendor through its central heavens
And I through wretched streets.

Deutsch, Babette. *Poetry Handbook*. Rev. ed. New York, Funk & Wagnalls, 1962.

A dictionary of terms with illustrations from English poetry and poetry in translation. The author is a poet, critic and teacher.

A *Prosody Handbook*. Ed. by Karl Shapiro and Robert Beum. New York, Harper & Row, 1965.

This is a compact manual dealing with the elements of prosody—line, meter, rhythm, rhyme and its uses, stanza forms, etc.

There are many fine collections of poetry. A few of the best-known general collections are:

Stevenson, Burton Egbert. *Home Book of Verse, American and English*. 9th ed. New York, Holt, 1953. 2 vols.

Stevenson, Burton Egbert. *Home Book of Modern Verse*. 2nd ed. New York, Holt, 1953.

Oxford Book of American Verse. Ed. by F. O. Matthiessen. New York, Oxford University Press, 1950.

Oxford Book of English Verse. Ed. by Sir Arthur Quiller-Couch. Oxford, Clarendon Press, 1939.

Untermeyer, Louis. *Modern American Poetry*. 8th ed. New York, Harcourt, 1962.

Untermeyer, Louis. *Modern British Poetry*. New and enl. ed. New York, Harcourt, 1962.

New York Times Book of Verse. Ed. by Thomas Lask. New York, Macmillan, 1970.

POLITICS, GOVERNMENT AND CURRENT EVENTS

T HOUGH MANY of the books listed here include historical information, most are annuals or are often revised and so contain up-to-date information on countries and governments. The following sources deal with the "necessary evil," as Thomas Paine called government.

THE WORLD

Council on Foreign Relations, Inc. *Political Handbook and Atlas of the World.* New York, Simon & Schuster, 1927-1968, 1970-.

This handbook, an annual except for 1969, lists rulers, political parties, cabinets, the press, etc., and when appropriate includes a brief "recent political events" for each country. Information is complete and compact and there is a map section at the end of the book.

The Worldmark Encyclopedia of Nations. 3rd rev. ed. New York, Worldmark Press, Harper & Row, 1967. 5 vols.

The five volumes in this set cover 1) the United Nations 2) Africa 3) the Americas 4) Asia and Australia 5) Europe. All aspects of a country are treated—trade, mining, forestry, banking, judicial system, etc. Though not issued annually (so note the copyright date for year of publication), it is a "practical guide to the geographic, historical, political, social and economic status" of nations and the U.N. There are some illustrations and small maps.

Europa Year Book. London, Europa Publications, 1946 to date. 2 vols. Annual.

Volume one includes international organizations and Europe. Volume two covers Africa, the Americas, Asia, Australia. Statistical information, constitution, diplomatic representation, the press, etc., are given for each country. For the tiny kingdom of Sikkim, for example, under the heading "Transport and Tourism" one learns that there is no railway or airport in Sikkim but there is an "Aerial Ropeway"—a ropeway, 13 miles long, which links the town of Gangtok to the foot of the Nathula Pass. (For complete information on education and learned societies see Europa's *World of Learning,* which is discussed in the education section.)

International Yearbook and Statesmen's Who's Who. London, Burke's Peerage, 1953 to date. Annual.

Includes information on international organizations and gives political, statistical and directory information on every country in the world. Biographical section contains sketches of world leaders.

Statesman's Year-Book. London, New York, Macmillan, 1864 to date. Annual.

Statesman's Year-Book has much statistical information and reliable facts on constitution, government, employment, finance, commerce, religion, education, diplomatic representation, etc., for all the countries of the world.

Wise, L. F. and Egan, E. W. *Kings, Rulers and Statesmen.* New York, Sterling, 1967.

An illustrated handbook giving, under the country name, a chronology of rulers and sometimes brief biographies.

Pearcy, G. Etzel, and Stoneman, Evelyn A. *A Handbook of New Nations.* New York, Crowell, 1968.

Offers the main features of sixty-one new nations. The handbook discusses history, government, economic and social conditions, and provides some maps.

Legum, Colon, ed. *Africa: A Handbook to the Continent.* Rev. enl. ed. New York, Praeger, 1966.

A one-volume work with a section on each nation and a section which treats the continent as a whole. Many illustrations and maps.

Yearbook of the United Nations. New York, United Nations Department of Public Information, 1947 to date. Annual.

A summary of the year's activities of the UN and its specialized agencies. It has a subject and a name index.

THE UNITED STATES

U.S. Congress. *Official Congressional Directory.* Washington, Government Printing Office, 1809 to date.

An indispensable work containing information on Congressional organization and personnel. Contains biographical sketches of Congressmen and officials, lists by state, committee memberships and information on various government commissions and boards. The directory also has maps of Congressional districts.

U.S. Congress. *Biographical Directory of the American Congress, 1774-1961.* Washington, Government Printing Office, 1961.

This directory lists Presidents, Cabinet officers and members of Congress, with brief biographies of each, from the 1st through the 86th Congresses.

United States Government Organization Manual. Washington, Government Printing Office, 1935 to date.

This is an annually revised manual on the federal government. It describes the creation, activities, organization (with charts of the more complex agencies) and chief officials of various departments and offices. It also includes quasi-official agencies like the National Academy of Sciences and the American National Red Cross.

The Book of the States. Chicago, Council of State Governments, 1935 to date.

Published every two years, this work gives information on state constitutions, elections, legislatures, etc. Also given are the nickname, motto, flower, bird and song for each state. (North Carolina's interesting state motto is: Esse Quam Videri—To Be Rather Than To Seem; the Pennsylvania state bird is the Ruffed Grouse; and Oklahoma's state flower is mistletoe . . . all year.) Supplements to the Book of States are issued to keep the lists of officials up-to-date.

Municipal Year Book. Chicago, International City Managers Association, 1934 to date.

This yearbook contains statistical data and information on U.S. cities. It discusses municipal problems and activities and gives a directory of chief officials for cities of 10,000 population or over, and of mayors and clerks for those of 5,000 to 10,000 populations.

Public Affairs Information Service. *Bulletin.* New York, Public Affairs Information Service, 1915 to date.

Known as PAIS, this is a subject index (somewhat like the *Readers' Guide*) to periodicals, pamphlets, government documents and even mimeographed material in economics, sociology, political science, government and legislation. Though not found in school libraries, it is important to know this tool exists and is available in all larger reference collections. It is issued weekly, cumulated at intervals and then issued in annual volumes.

Mitchell, Edwin Valentine. *An Encyclopedia of American Politics* New York, Doubleday, 1946. Reprint: New York, Greenwood Press, 1968.

Useful for its identification of terms, slogans, nicknames, biographies of political figures, and the work also has excerpts from significant documents.

America Votes; A Handbook of Contemporary American Election Statistics. Ed. by Richard M. Scammon. v. 1-2 New York, Macmillan, 1956, 1958. v. 3-6 Pittsburgh, University of Pittsburgh Press, 1959-1966. v. 7- Washington, Congressional Quarterly, 1968-   . Biennial.

Arranged alphabetically by state, the Scammon books contain valuable statistics on the vote since 1945 for president, governor, senator, and congressman. These volumes include maps of state counties and congressional districts and of assembly districts for large cities.

Davis, John P. *The American Negro Reference Book.* Englewood Cliffs, N.J., Prentice-Hall, 1966.

Current social, cultural, economic aspects of American Negro life are discussed in this book.

The Negro Handbook. Compiled by the editors of Ebony. Chicago, Johnson, 1966.

Factual and statistical information is presented to document the current status of blacks in the United States. Biographical information is included as well as an annotated list of works on the Negro.

Klein, Bernard, and Icolari, Daniel, eds. *Reference Encyclopedia of the American Indian.* New York, Bernard Klein, 1967.

A source book for information on contemporary American Indian affairs. Though it includes brief biographical information on contemporary American Indians and people working in Indian affairs, it consists primarily of lists of government agencies, museums, libraries, reservations, etc.

Petersen, Svend. *A Statistical History of the American Presidential Elections.* New York, Frederick Ungar, 1963.

Statistical compilations of various aspects of the vote for each presidential election from 1789 to 1960 are found in this work. Tables are arranged by election year, by state, by political party, etc., as illustrated below.

Election of 1860

TABLE 21   Electoral and Popular Vote

States	L	Br	Bl	D	Lincoln	Douglas	Breck.	Bell	Smith
Alabama		9				13,651	48,831	27,875	
Arkansas		4				5,227	28,732	20,094	
California	4				39,173	38,516	34,334	6,817	
Connecticut	6				43,486	17,364	16,558	3,337	
Delaware			3		3,816	1,069	7,344	3,868	
Florida			3			367	8,543	5,437	
Georgia		10				11,613	52,131	43,050	
Illinois	11				172,171	160,205	2,402	4,913	35
Indiana	13				139,033	115,509	12,295	5,306	
Iowa	4				70,409	55,111	1,048	1,763	
Kentucky			12		1,364	25,651	53,143	66,058	
Louisiana		6				7,625	22,681	20,204	
Maine	8				62,811	26,693	6,368	2,046	
Maryland		8			2,895	5,953	42,511	41,875	
Massachusetts	13				106,649	34,492	6,277	22,536	
Michigan	6				88,480	65,057	805	405	
Minnesota	4				22,069	11,920	748	62	
Mississippi		7				3,283	40,797	25,040	
Missouri				9	17,028	58,801	31,317	58,372	
New Hampshire	5				37,519	25,881	2,112	441	
New Jersey	4			3	58,346	62,869			
New York	35				362,646	312,510			
North Carolina		10				2,701	48,539	44,990	
Ohio	23				231,610	187,232	11,405	12,194	136
Oregon	3				5,496	4,127	5,342	976	
Pennsylvania	27				268,030	16,765	178,871	12,776	
Rhode Island	4				12,240	7,753			1
South Carolina		8							
Tennessee			12			11,428	66,440	70,706	
Texas		4					47,548	15,438	
Vermont	5				33,888	8,748	1,859	217	
Virginia			15		1,929	16,292	74,379	74,701	
Wisconsin	5				86,110	65,021	888	161	
TOTALS	180	72	39	12	1,867,198	1,379,434	854,248	591,658	172

The card catalog of your library will under subject headings reveal recent books which, though not specifically "reference books," may be used to find current factual information. Two examples are:

Cahn, E. S. ed. *Our Brother's Keeper: The Indian in White America.* Cleveland, World, 1969.

Steiner, Stan. *La Raza: the Mexican Americans.* New York, Harper & Row, 1970.

The daily newspapers and magazines, discussed in another chapter, are common tools for keeping informed of the latest news and of what governments are toppling and which ones are reelecting. Here are two other good sources; both describe and index current events.

Facts on File: a weekly world news digest with cumulative index. New York, Facts on File, 1940 to date. Weekly with annual cumulations.

This digest of news is arranged under such headings as World Affairs, National Affairs, Finance, Economy, Science, Education, etc. It also covers events in the arts, listing books published and theatre openings, has obituaries, and includes the latest in sports. An important and useful guide to current information. *(Keesing's Contemporary Archives* is a British work similar to *Facts on File.* It is also a weekly, indexed diary of world events.)

FACTS ON FILE (FOF) **A**
WORLD NEWS DIGEST WITH INDEX
© 1970 by Facts on File, Inc.   Reg. U.S. Pat. Off.
Published Weekly
Vol. XXX, No. 1552   July 23–29, 1970

THIS WEEK

World Affairs
U.A.R., Jordan accepted U.S. peace plan for Middle East; Syria, Iraq, Palestinian commandos refused it; Israel sought further guarantees. **B**
U.S.S.R., West Germany began talks on treaty renunciating use of force.
South Africa arms sale controversy; U.N. met on issue.
U.S. proposal before SALT talks; other disarmament, atomic energy news.
Pages 529–533

National Affairs
Report on campus unrest sent to President Nixon; FBI report said Kent State shootings were unnecessary; hearings on campus unrest. **C**
Congress passed education funds bill, D.C. crime bill; House panel charged coverup on Mylai.
National goals panel issued report; President visited cities in West.
Pages 533–535

Congressional Quarterly Weekly Report. Washington, D.C., Congressional Quarterly Inc., 1945 to date.

CQ is a weekly service (with a quarterly index) giving information on U.S. Congressional activities. It also publishes a yearly almanac which "distills, reorganizes and cross-indexes" the year in Congress. It is very helpful when searching for action on bills, the voting records of members of Congress, presidential messages, etc. (Other sources of information on Congress and the U.S. Government are described in detail in guides to U.S. Government publications, some of which are in the suggested reading list in the back of this book.)

LAWS

Zinn, Charles J. *How Our Laws Are Made.* Washington, Government Printing Office, 1969.

This best selling government pamphlet (available for 35¢ from the Superintendent of Documents, U.S. Government Printing Office, Washington, D.C., 20402) gives a careful explanation of the complicated legislative process. Because it is in paperback it may be kept by libraries in the pamphlet file (called a "vertical file") so if it is not found in the catalog ask the librarian for it. (A simple and graphic explanation of this subject is also given in the *World Book Encyclopedia* under "United States, Government of" in an article titled "How a bill becomes a law.")

No attempt is made here to explain all sources of government legislative information except to indicate the kind of material which is available. For detailed descriptions see the Schmeckebier and Easton book, *Government Publications and Their Use,* and other works recommended in the bibliography to this guide on page 185.

When laws are passed by Congress they are first printed individually in pamphlet form known as "slip laws." At the end of each year they are published by the Government Printing Office as *United States Statutes at Large*. These are primarily of research interest because many laws modify earlier ones and are themselves modified by later legislation.

To find current laws use:

U.S. Laws, Statutes, etc. United States Code, 1964 edition. Washington, Government Printing Office, 1965.

This multi-volume set is the official compilation of all laws in force as of January 3, 1965. The *U.S. Code* is usually issued every six years and cumulative supplements are issued after each session of Congress. (There are commercially publishd editions known as *United States Code Annotated*. These editions include notes on judicial interpretation of the law as well as the law itself.)

U.S. Congress. *Congressional Record*. Washington, Government Printing Office, 1873 to date.

The *Record* is a newspaper issued every day Congress is in session and there is nothing quite like it. It is all things—funny, serious, lofty and low-down. It contains words spoken on the floors of both chambers (such as speeches and debate on legislation), and much that is not said since members may add revised and extended remarks and letters, news articles and other items. Often things are included by a Congressman so he can have them reprinted and distributed back home under the *Congressional Record* banner. The *Record* is bound and indexed (by name and subject) at the end of each session and a "History of Bills and Resolutions" index is included.

QUOTATIONS

Q<small>UOTATIONS</small> are best used sparingly amid original thought. Books of quotations are reference works in which one can find the sayings of a particular person, verify or identify a particular quotation and find quotations on a particular subject. These books are especially "democratic," including something as familiar as "snug as a bug in a rug" along with the lofty expressions of a Supreme Court Justice. A few of the basic, general sources are described here.

Bartlett, John. *Familiar Quotations.* 14th ed. rev. and enl. Boston, Little, Brown 1968.

One of the best standard collections, Bartlett's is arranged chronologically by authors quoted and has an excellent key word index. The following quotation by Benjamin Franklin can be found in the index under several key words—eagle, turkey, bird, moral and material welfare.

> I wish the bald eagle had not been chosen as the representative of our country; he is a bird of bad moral character; like those among men who live by sharping and robbing, he is generally poor, and often very lousy.
>
> The turkey is a much more respectable bird, and withal a true original native of America.
>
> **Letter to Sarah Bache**
> [*January 26, 1784*]

Stevenson, Burton Egbert. *Home Book of Quotations.* 9th ed. rev. Dodd, 1958.

This is a very comprehensive quotation book arranged by subject and with an index. It covers classical and modern quotations. It you look under the heading "study" you will find the following advice from J. M. Barrie:

> "Concentrate though your coat-tails be on fire."

The same editor has compiled several quotation books such as the *Home Book of Shakespeare Quotations* (New York, Scribner, 1937) the *Home Book of Bible Quotations* (New York, Harper, 1949) and the *Home Book of Proverbs, Maxims and Familiar Phrases* (New York, Macmillan, 1948).

Other excellent sources are:

Hoyt, Jehiel Keeler. *Hoyt's New Cyclopedia of Practical Quotations.* compl. by Kate Louise Roberts. New York, Funk & Wagnalls, 1922.

Oxford Dictionary of Quotations. 2nd ed. London, New York, Oxford University Press, 1953.

Simpson, James Beasley. *Contemporary Quotations.* New York, Crowell, 1964.

Evans, Bergen. *Dictionary of Quotations.* New York, Delacorte Press, 1968.

It saves time if you always check the arrangement in quotation books. When looking for quotations by a specific person it's easier to use a book arranged by author or speaker; at other times you might need sayings on a particular subject so an alphabetical list by subject is the most useful. Good quotation books have indexes covering the approaches not used in the basic arrangement.

SCIENCE

Science, as the last and probably endless frontier, boasts a staggering amount of published information. Listed here are general works, broad in scope. Not listed are the thousands of books on specific areas within the field of science.

GENERAL WORKS

McGraw-Hill Encyclopedia of Science and Technology. Rev. ed. New York, McGraw-Hill, 1966. 15 vols.

This international reference work is comprehensive and scholarly though it is aimed at the intelligent layman. There are introductory survey articles for each branch of science as well as articles on more specific topics. Bibliographies follow the longer articles. Biographies are not included. Volume 15 is the index to this indispensible set and, most important in such a changing field, the set is kept up to date by an annual, the *McGraw-Hill Yearbook of Science and Technology.*

Van Nostrand's Scientific Encyclopedia. 4th ed. Princeton, N.J., Van Nostrand, 1968.

A single alphabetical arrangement covering all science from aeronautics to zoology. There are articles on the centipede, the measles, nitric acid and for the airplane buff a discussion of "wing stress analysis."

Graham, E. C. *The Basic Dictionary of Science.* New York, Macmillan. 1965.

A dictionary followed by lists of abbreviations used in science, chemical elements with their atomic weights and numbers, Greek letters, Roman numerals, and tables showing the classification of plants and animals and other related scientific information.

Harper Encyclopedia of Science. 2nd rev. ed. Ed. by James R. Newman. New York, Harper & Row, 1967.

Harper's is an excellent, readable one-volume encyclopedia covering a wide range of topics from the principles of the new math to the courtship of fish. Biographies are included. The index and many illustrations contribute to its value. Here is a sample:

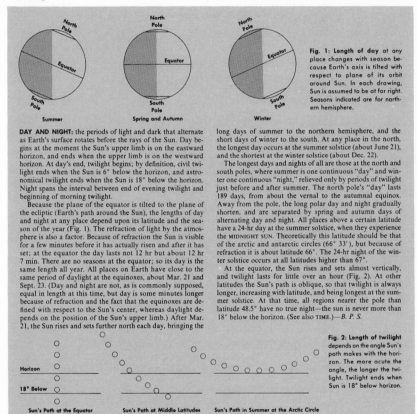

Fig. 1: Length of day at any place changes with season because Earth's axis is tilted with respect to plane of its orbit around Sun. In each drawing, Sun is assumed to be at far right. Seasons indicated are for northern hemisphere.

DAY AND NIGHT: the periods of light and dark that alternate as Earth's surface rotates before the rays of the Sun. Day begins at the moment the Sun's upper limb is on the eastward horizon, and ends when the upper limb is on the westward horizon. At day's end, twilight begins; by definition, civil twilight ends when the Sun is 6° below the horizon, and astronomical twilight ends when the Sun is 18° below the horizon. Night spans the interval between end of evening twilight and beginning of morning twilight.

Because the plane of the equator is tilted to the plane of the ecliptic (Earth's path around the Sun), the lengths of day and night at any place depend upon its latitude and the season of the year (Fig. 1). The refraction of light by the atmosphere is also a factor. Because of refraction the Sun is visible for a few minutes before it has actually risen and after it has set; at the equator the day lasts not 12 hr but about 12 hr 7 min. There are no seasons at the equator; so its day is the same length all year. All places on Earth have close to the same period of daylight at the equinoxes, about Mar. 21 and Sept. 23. (Day and night are not, as is commonly supposed, equal in length at this time, but day is some minutes longer because of refraction and the fact that the equinoxes are defined with respect to the Sun's center, whereas daylight depends on the position of the Sun's upper limb.) After Mar. 21, the Sun rises and sets further north each day, bringing the

long days of summer to the northern hemisphere, and the short days of winter to the south. At any place in the north, the longest day occurs at the summer solstice (about June 21), and the shortest at the winter solstice (about Dec. 22).

The longest days and nights of all are those at the north and south poles, where summer is one continuous "day" and winter one continuous "night," relieved only by periods of twilight just before and after summer. The north pole's "day" lasts 189 days, from about the vernal to the autumnal equinox. Away from the pole, the long polar day and night gradually shorten, and are separated by spring and autumn days of alternating day and night. All places above a certain latitude have a 24-hr day at the summer solstice, when they experience the MIDNIGHT SUN. Theoretically this latitude should be that of the arctic and antarctic circles (66° 33'), but because of refraction it is about latitude 66°. The 24-hr night of the winter solstice occurs at all latitudes higher than 67°.

At the equator, the Sun rises and sets almost vertically, and twilight lasts for little over an hour (Fig. 2). At other latitudes the Sun's path is oblique, so that twilight is always longer, increasing with latitude, and being longest at the summer solstice. At that time, all regions nearer the pole than latitude 48.5° have no true night—the sun is never more than 18° below the horizon. (See also TIME.)—*B. P. S.*

Fig. 2: Length of twilight depends on the angle Sun's path makes with the horizon. The more acute the angle, the longer the twilight. Twilight ends when Sun is 18° below horizon.

Asimov, Isaac. *The New Intelligent Man's Guide to Science.* New York, Basic Books, 1965.

Another one-volume, lively work which makes many complicated subjects understandable. Part I deals with the physical sciences and Part II covers the biological sciences.

FROM: *The Way Things Work.*

WHY DOES A SHIP FLOAT?

According to Archimedes' principle, a body which is wholly or partly immersed in a fluid undergoes a loss in weight equal to the weight of fluid which it displaces. An aluminium cube with sides 1 ft. in length weighs about 168 lb. (Fig. 1a). A cubic foot of water weighs about 62 lb. If the aluminium cube is immersed in water (Fig. 1b), its weight has apparently decreased to 106 lb. This is because the cube displaces a cubic foot of water and thereby undergoes a loss in weight equal to the weight of this displaced water. The upward force due to *buoyancy* in this case is equal to 62 lb. and acts at the centre of gravity of the displaced volume of water. If a body, on being totally immersed in a fluid, would displace a volume of fluid whose weight is greater than that of the body concerned, then that body will float on the fluid. Floating merely means that the body sinks into the fluid to such a depth that the displaced volume of fluid weighs exactly as much as the whole floating body. In that case the upward force (buoyancy), which is equal to the weight of the displaced fluid, is in equilibrium with the weight of the body. A 1 ft. wooden cube weighs about 50 lb. It will float in water; the submerged part of the cube displaces a volume of water weighing 50 lb., so that the upward force is 50 lb. and thus counter-balances the weight of the cube (Fig. 2). Hence the displacement of a floating object is equal to its weight.

This is the elementary principle of floating. However, a ship must additionally have stability, i.e., it must be able to right itself after being swung to an inclined position by an external force such as wind pressure. A ship is said to "heel" when it leans over to port or starboard (Fig. 3a); the term "trim" refers to the longitudinal position of a ship in relation to the waterline: the ship is said to be trimmed by the head (as in Fig. 3b) or by the stern, according as the head or the stern lies deeper down in the water. Stability is especially important with regard to the danger of capsizing. Fig. 4a shows the ship in its normal position. Its weight can be conceived as a downward force acting at its centre of gravity S. The counterbalancing upward force acts at the centre of buoyancy W, which is the centre of gravity of the displaced volume of water. Normally the points S and W are located on the same vertical line. When the ship heels over (Figs 4b and 4c), the centre of buoyancy shifts to a different position (marked W^1), and the upward force acting here strives to rotate the ship around its centre of gravity S. The intersection M of the line of action of the upward force A with the ship's axis of symmetry is called the metacentre. If the metacentre is located above the centre of gravity S of the ship (as in Fig. 4b), the ship will return to its normal upright position; it is said to be in stable equilibrium. On the other hand, if the metacentre is below the centre of gravity S (Fig. 4c), the ship is in unstable equilibrium and will capsize when it heels over.

The Way Things Work. New York, Simon and Schuster, 1967.

Much of this is on an advanced level but the clear language (translated from the original German) and the illustrations help. Its subtitle is "An Illustrated Encyclopedia of Technology," and the book deals with a variety of subjects such as color television, pumps, dry ice, mirrors, cameras and fire extinguishers. See the text and the illustration above and on the following page for a sample of the format used for each subject:

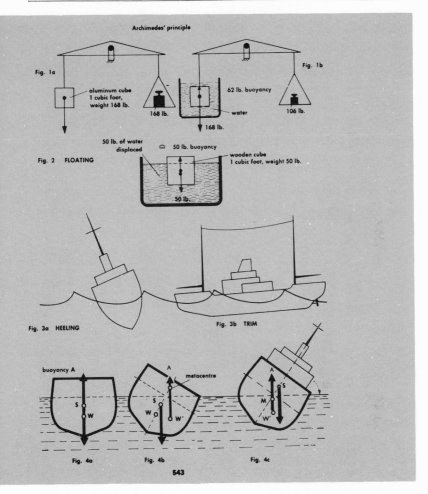

Archimedes' principle

Fig. 1a

aluminum cube
1 cubic foot,
weight 168 lb.

168 lb.

Fig. 1b

62 lb. buoyancy

water

106 lb.

168 lb.

50 lb. of water
displaced

Fig. 2   FLOATING

50 lb. buoyancy

wooden cube
1 cubic foot, weight 50 lb.

50 lb.

Fig. 3a HEELING

Fig. 3b TRIM

buoyancy A

A

metacentre

S

W

S

W

W'

A

S

M

W'

Fig. 4a

Fig. 4b

Fig. 4c

543

Gamow, George. *One, Two, Three . . . Infinity: Facts and Specu-lations of Science.* New York, Viking Press, 1961.

Here is a delightful book written by a nuclear physicist who is that rare combination of scientist and writer who can com-municate his knowledge to the layman. It is entertaining and conveys the endless possibilities of science. Subjects discussed include what the author describes as the "Law of Disorder" and "Modern Alchemy."

137

SUBJECT AREAS

Handbook of Chemistry and Physics. 51st ed. Ed. by Robert C. Weast. Ed. in charge of mathematics, Samuel M. Selby. Cleveland, Ohio, Chemical Rubber.

A ready-reference book, revised almost annually, of chemical and physical data and giving definitions, tables and formulas.

Menzel, Donald H. *Field Guide to the Stars and Planets.* Boston, Houghton Mifflin, 1964. (The Peterson Field Guide Series)

A guide by the director of the Harvard College Observatory which includes information on stars, planets, the moon, satellites, comets. The book is well illustrated with "sky maps" and such, and describes features like Haley's Comet and an eclipse of the sun and the moon. Here is an example of this small book's pithiness:

Aberration of Light. A person walking rapidly through a heavy rainstorm with the drops falling straight downward, will have to tilt his umbrella slightly forward to compensate for his own motion (Fig. 61). In the same way and for the same reason, an astronomer on the rapidly moving earth must tilt his telescope slightly forward in the direction of the earth's motion in order to have the starlight fall exactly down the center of his tube. As a result of this motion, the apparent position of a star does not ordinarily coincide with its true position. We term this phenomenon the *aberration* or "wandering" of light. The maximum shift from true to apparent position is 20˝.47.

Fig. 61. Aberration of light

Henderson, I. F., and Henderson, W. D. *Dictionary of Biological Terms*. 8th ed. Ed. by J. H. Kenneth. Princeton, N.J., Van Nostrand, 1963.

The "pronunciation, derivation, and definition of terms in biology, botany, zoology, anatomy, cytology, genetics, embryology and physiology."

Challinor, John. *A Dictionary of Geology*. 2nd ed. New York, Oxford University Press, 1964.

This dictionary defines terms and examines concepts. Many entries have quotations illustrating meanings. There is even a word, "clunch," which is defined as "an old local name for various stiff clays."

Dorland's Illustrated Medical Dictionary. 24th ed. Philadelphia, W. B. Saunders, 1965.

A standard dictionary in the field of medicine.

Modell, Walter, and others. *Drugs*. New York, Time, Inc., 1967.

Drugs, their origins, use, and misuse. Sample headings include: "Poisons That Save Lives," "Alcohol: The Oldest Drug," and "Mind Influencers."

BIOGRAPHY

World Who's Who In Science. Chicago, Marquis, 1968.

A world list from antiquity to the present day. It has the brief paragraphs typical of all the "Who's Who" books.

(See chapter on biographical sources for a Who's Who sample and for information on *American Men of Science*.)

Asimov, Isaac. *Asimov's Biographical Encyclopedia of Science and Technology*. Garden City, N.Y., Doubleday, 1964.

Biographies are not in alphabetical order. They're arranged chronologically to show the influence of outstanding scientists upon their followers. Covers scientists from the Age of Greece to the Space Age. Below, an example of the detailed but informal style, the beginning of the biography of American physicist Robert H. Goddard.

[414] **GODDARD,** Robert Hutchings
American physicist
Born: Worcester, Massachusetts,
October 5, 1882
Died: Baltimore, Maryland, August 10, 1945

Goddard was raised in Boston, a sickly boy whose thoughts turned inward toward what seemed fantasy in those days. His family returned to Worcester when he was sixteen and he went to the Polytechnic Institute there, graduating in 1908. He received his Ph.D. in physics at Clark University in Worcester in 1911. He taught at Princeton but returned to Clark in 1914 and remained there for nearly thirty years.

He had a mind daring enough for a science fiction writer, and he was firmly grounded in science, to boot. While still an undergraduate, he described a railway line between Boston and New York in which the trains traveled in a vacuum under the pull of an electromagnetic field and completed their trip in ten minutes. He called it "Traveling in 1950," but, alas, the railroad trip still took four hours and more when 1950 actually rolled around.

He also grew interested in rocketry as a teenager; by 1919 this interest had ripened to the point where he published a small book entitled *A Method of Reaching Extreme Altitudes.* In this he had been anticipated by Tsiolkovsky [341b], but Goddard went a step further and began to experiment with ordinary gunpowder rockets.

In 1923 Goddard tested the first of a new type of rocket engine, one using liquid fuels, gasoline, and liquid oxygen. This was his first revolutionary advance over previous solid-fuel rockets. (Of course, early rockets were used mostly in Fourth of July celebrations and similar affairs, but there had been a time in the first half of the nineteenth century when they were used in warfare. Our national anthem speaks of "the rockets' red glare.")

In 1926 Goddard sent up his first rocket. His wife took a picture of him standing next to it before it was launched. It was about four feet high, six inches in diameter, and was held in a frame like a child's jungle gym. This, nevertheless, was the grandfather of the monsters that a generation later were to rumble upward from the Transcaspian, from Florida, and from California.

Goddard managed to get a few thousand dollars from the Smithsonian Institution and in July 1929 sent up a larger

The Scientific American Book of Projects for the Amateur Scientist. C. L. Strong. New York, Simon & Schuster, 1960.

An example of several available books which describe science projects. This one covers everything from the making of a simple telescope and a sundial to growing algae on a window shelf.

Applied Science and Technology Index. New York, H. W. Wilson, 1958 to date.

An index to articles appearing in technical and scientific magazines. It is used like the *Reader's Guide to Periodical Literature* (see chapter on Newspapers and Magazines) which also indexes a few science magazines.

SPEECHES

ORATORY, that old fashioned form of communication, continues to inspire, incite, or alienate listeners. Speeches are another approach to history.

Peterson, Houston. *Treasury of the World's Great Speeches.* Rev. and enl. ed. New York, Simon & Schuster, 1965.
   A few of the speeches included in this world history collection are:
> Sermon on the Mount
> Napoleon Bids Farewell to the Old Guard
> John F. Kennedy's Inaugural Address
> Martin Luther King, Jr. "I have a dream . . ."

Hurd, Charles. *A Treasury of Great American Speeches.* New York, Hawthorn Books, 1959.
   Texts of speeches reflecting American history are preceded by brief "news stories" which set the scene and describe the circumstances. When pertinent a "sequel" describes what happened after the speech was given. Includes Patrick Henry—naturally—and many others such as Oliver Wendell Holmes, Billy Sunday, Woodrow Wilson, and J. Robert Oppenheimer.

New York Times Index
   The newspaper often prints the full texts of contemporary (though now perhaps historical) speeches and documents, which may later be included in anthologies. (See chapter on Newspapers and Magazines for full details on this index.)

Vital Speeches of the Day. New York, City News Pub. Co., 1934 to date. Biweekly.
   This magazine prints the full texts of important contemporary speeches given by leaders in all fields. It carries the slogan "Best thought of the best minds on current national questions."

The cover of each issue carries the table of contents and indicates the wide variety of speakers, as seen in this sample:

SPORTS, RECREATION AND HOBBIES

Rᴇᴍᴇᴍʙᴇʀ that this is a brief general list of only a few of the books that have been written about almost every sport or game you can think of.

Menke, Frank G. *Encyclopedia of Sports.* 4th rev. ed. New York, A. S. Barnes, 1968.

A reference book which has records, history and rules of a wide variety of sports including, to name just a few, baseball, croquet, polo, tennis and weight lifting. It also has miscellaneous information such as a list of stadiums with their seating capacities. Some of the history includes the surprising fact that billiards requires so much physical training:

> A billiardist is aware that his leg muscles must be perfectly attuned since, during a prolonged period of play, he may be forced to walk from 1 to 3 miles, going to the table to make his shot, walking around it, walking back to his seat when he misses and to resume when his opponent has failed. Since the player's activities demand considerable leaning when shooting, he needs abdominal muscles that can stand the ultimate in strain. The muscles of the player's shoulders, arms and hands must be at their best.
>
> Some billiardists, to acquire fitness for a match, spend hours in gymnasiums. Others take daily runs on the road or walk swiftly over long routes. They practice bending exercises, twirl objects to aid the muscles in the forearms and wrists, and go through long sieges of spasmodic squeezing of a small ball, or a similar object, to strengthen their finger muscles.

and some incidental background on bobsledding:

> The bobsled was developed from the sled of ancient times, which was merely a strip of animal skin stretched between smoothed strips of wood acting as runners. The first step in this evolution was the toboggan. It was conceived and developed about 1890 by a group of thrill-seeking American and English vacationers in Switzerland who were looking for something more daring than plodding through the Swiss Alps on snowshoes.
>
> They laid out a course on the mountains around St. Moritz and were soon hurtling down the snow-clad slopes.
>
> It soon was discovered that the toboggan was too safe for this particular brand of daredevils, so they came up with the idea of mounting the toboggan on sled-like runners. This produced speeds far in excess of what the toboggan was capable of doing, but the light weight of the toboggan-sled, combined with the excessive speeds, caused the sled to lose its course and there were many serious accidents and some deaths.

The Baseball Encyclopedia: The Complete and Official Record of Major League Baseball. New York, Macmillan, 1969.

A compilation listing season by season and lifetime statistical records of everyone who has played major league baseball. It covers the game from the beginning through 1968 and gives data on pitchers, players, managers, World Series and All-Star games. The total picture of the game.

Hollander, Zander, ed. *The Modern Encyclopedia of Basketball.* New York, Four Winds: Scholastic, 1969.

Basketball started one day in 1891 when "Doc" Naismith nailed a peach basket at either end of a gymnasium and tossed his gym class a soccer ball. Historical and contemporary information is included in this comprehensive book.

Treat, Roger. *The Official Encyclopedia of Football.* 6th rev. ed. New York, A. S. Barnes, 1968.

Includes information on players, coaches, teams, leagues, a year-by-year history and a description of the evolution of the game.

Bancroft, Jesse H. *Games*. Rev. enl. ed. New York, Macmillan, 1938 (1967 39th printing).

This is a complete book of games "for the playground, home, school and gymnasium." The index is a page guide but also indicates whether the game is suited for students in the elementary grades, junior or senior high school, or college and whether the game is played by one person or more than one. It covers social and quiet games, games for track and field, beanbag games, singing games, stunts and contests. That is, everything from hop scotch to magic to the javelin throw.

Foster, Robert Frederick. *Foster's Complete Hoyle*. Rev. ed. Philadelphia, Lippincott, 1963.

An encyclopedia of indoor games—especially card games and games of chance. Hoyle gives the rules and techniques of everything from bridge and poker to dominoes and checkers. It even explains (under the heading "Juvenile Games") Old Maid, Pig, and Go Fish.

This is the origin of the phrase "played according to Hoyle," meaning, of course, played in accordance with the rules of the game. The book includes many versions of Solitaire in case you're bored with the one you know, and states that even in this game there is an "opponent:"

> BY Solitaire or Patience is meant any card game that can be played by one person. His opponent is the luck of the shuffle—or any personification thereof he chooses to pose, as Beelzebub.

Salny, Roslyn W. *Hobby Collections A-Z*. New York, Crowell, 1965.

A work which gives the techniques of organizing and pursuing a collection such as autographs, menus, postcards, stamps, road maps, etc. Stamp collections are quite common but this book suggests a collection of postmarks and in the brief orientation and history of this hobby says:

"One of the most interesting foreign postmarks was devised in France, during the siege of Paris by the Prussian Army in 1870. Paris was cut off from the outside world, and carrier pigeons and large postal balloons provided the only means of communication. Letters that traveled by balloon were postmarked Par Ballon Monté, "carried by balloon."

Scott's Standard Postage Stamp Catalogue. New York, Scott Publications, 1867 to date. Annual.

An encyclopedia of philately giving illustrations, description, denominations and value of major stamps of all countries.

Carson, R. A. G. *Coins of the World.* New York, Harper, 1962.

A world history of coins from ancient times to the present. It also includes a section on tokens and other objects which resemble coins, such as one from early Rome which might have been issued as some form of ticket for the Roman games.

Reinfeld, Fred. *Catalogue of the World's Most Popular Coins.* Rev. by Burton Hobson. Garden City, N.Y., Doubleday, 1967.

This source lists coins with illustrations of each. Value in U.S. dollars is given for each and where coins are not silver their composition is given. Some early American coins were for odd amounts such as the Half Cent, Half Dime, Three Cents coin, and one for Twenty Cents.

Hewitt James. *A Practical Guide to Yoga.* New York, Funk and Wagnalls, 1968.

Subtitled "a systematic program of meditations and exercises—the natural way to health and vitality," this offers an alternative (or a supplement) to more violent exercise and is an example of the wide variety of books on health. Illustrations demonstrate the yoga postures.

PART III

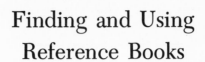

Finding and Using
Reference Books

THE LIBRARY AND ITS CARD CATALOG

TERMS AND ABBREVIATIONS USED IN REFERENCE MATERIAL

FOOTNOTES AND BIBLIOGRAPHY

A FEW WORDS ON WRITING A PAPER

SAMPLE TERM PAPER

THE LIBRARY AND
ITS CARD CATALOG

T HE GIANT STEP forward in any reference project is familiarity with the library and an understanding of the library card catalog.

CLASSIFICATION SYSTEM

Books are arranged within the library according to a classification system. They are classified or sorted into groups so that books on the same subject are located together.

DEWEY DECIMAL CLASSIFICATION: FIRST SUMMARY[1]		LIBRARY OF CONGRESS CLASSIFICATION	
		A	General works—polygraphy
000	General works	B	Philosophy—religion
		C	History—auxiliary sciences
100	Philosophy	D	History and topography (except America)
200	Religion	E-F	America
		G	Geography—anthropology
300	Social sceinces	H	Social sciences
		J	Political science
		K	Law
400	Language	L	Education
		M	Music
500	Pure science	N	Fine arts
		P	Language and literature
600	Technology	Q	Science
		R	Medicine
700	The arts	S	Agriculture—plant and animal industry
		T	Technology
800	Literature	U	Military science
		V	Naval science
900	History	Z	Bibliography and library science

There are two main classification systems used by libraries: the Dewey Decimal System (used in most libraries because it can be easily adapted to the needs of a small book collection) and the system of the Library of Congress (used in very large collections because it allows for greater subdivisions without making lengthy class numbers). These two systems are divided into the main groups illustrated on the opposite page.

Within each of these large groups there are further divisions indicated by numbers or letters.

In the Dewey system, for example, the 900s are shown above as the identification for history. But within that, 940 is the number for European history and 973 begins American history. And within the 973s you will find still more divisions such as:

973	American History
973.1	American discovery & exploration
973.2	American Colonial Period
973.3	American Revolution
973.4	American Constitutional Period
973.5	Early 19th Century America
973.6	Middle 19th Century America
973.7	American Civil War

and so on into the 20th century. That's how it works. You don't need to remember it. Use the card catalog to get the number.

CALL NUMBER

The location of a book in the library is determined by the call number. The call number is a combination of the subject classification number and a letter or letter number indicating the author. The *Encyclopedia of the American Revolution* by Mark M. Boatner might have this call number: 973.3
B
or in larger libraries a more precise author identification: 973.3
B63

which will appear on the spine of the book and on the cards in the catalog which refer to that book. Books are arranged on the shelves according to number and then alphabetically by the author's name.

CARD CATALOG

Depending on the classification system, the size of the collection (and perhaps the whim of the person assigning the numbers), a book may be given different numbers in different libraries so always check the card catalog. Often fiction (though usually alphabetically by author) and biographies (though usually alphabetically by biographee) are treated differently from library to library.

The card catalog shows what books the library has and where you will find them.

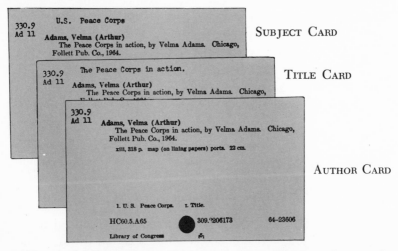

There are three kinds of cards in the catalog: author cards, title cards, and subject cards, usually arranged in one alphabet. So you have three approaches to locating a book if you know the author, title or subject you want.

The most complete information is given on the author card, where you will find:

the call number of the book
the author's name
title and subtitle
the name of the publisher
copyright date or date of publication

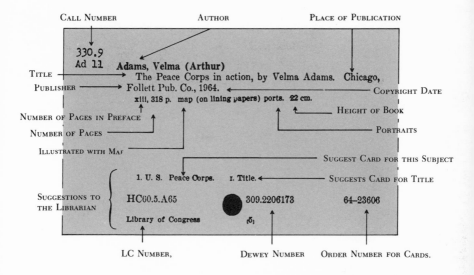

CALL NUMBER   AUTHOR   PLACE OF PUBLICATION

330.9
Ad 11   **Adams, Velma (Arthur)**
    The Peace Corps in action, by Velma Adams.   Chicago,
    Follett Pub. Co., 1964.
    xiii, 318 p.   map (on lining papers) ports. 22 cm.

TITLE
PUBLISHER
COPYRIGHT DATE
NUMBER OF PAGES IN PREFACE
NUMBER OF PAGES
HEIGHT OF BOOK
ILLUSTRATED WITH MAP
PORTRAITS

     SUGGEST CARD FOR THIS SUBJECT

    1. U. S. Peace Corps.   I. Title.   SUGGESTS CARD FOR TITLE

SUGGESTIONS TO
THE LIBRARIAN

    HC60.5.A65   ●   309.2206173   64–23606

    Library of Congress   ₅₁

LC NUMBER,   DEWEY NUMBER   ORDER NUMBER FOR CARDS.

When person, place, subject and title are the same the arrangement (usually) is as follows:

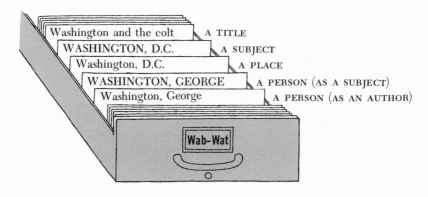

Washington and the colt   A TITLE
WASHINGTON, D.C.   A SUBJECT
Washington, D.C.   A PLACE
WASHINGTON, GEORGE   A PERSON (AS A SUBJECT)
Washington, George   A PERSON (AS AN AUTHOR)

Wab–Wat

151

The card catalog also has "see" and "see also" references (as discussed in the use of periodical and newspaper indexes). A sample of a "see" reference—a direction from a heading not used to the heading used:

PEACE CORPS

see

U.S. Peace Corps

A sample of a "see also" reference—a direction to related material:

GHOSTS

see also

Demonology

Spiritualism

Superstition

ALPHABETIZATION

Knowing the alphabet does not mean you're home free. Alphabetization for indexes and filing cards has two major systems. One is a word by word system (as used in the Encyclopedia Americana) and the other is a letter by letter system (as used in the Encyclopedia Britannica) where each entry, no matter how many words, is treated as though it spelled one word.

Word by Word	*Letter by Letter*
West Point	Western Union
West York, Pa.	Westminster Abbey
Western Union	West Point
Westminster Abbey	Westward Ho!
Westward Ho!	West York, Pa.
Wheat	Wheat
Wheat germ	Wheatear (bird)
Wheatear (bird)	Wheat germ

Filing of names, especially foreign names, is complicated but three common stumbling blocks are:

The St., in for example St. Valentine's Day, is usually filed as though spelled out: Saint Valentine's Day.

Names beginning with Mc are sometimes filed ahead of all the M's, sometimes filed as though spelled Mac, and sometimes filed as Mc in a letter by letter style.

Prefixes such as Lord, Mrs., Viscount are usually ignored in filing: Long, *Mrs.* Adam

Long, *Baron* Paul

If you can't find something you expect to find in a certain source or in the card catalog, check the instructions, try an alphabet variation, or ask for assistance.

Only the most common arrangements and catalog cards are discussed here. There are many variations on basic classification systems (as mentioned in the classifying and filing of biographies) and there are other kinds of catalog cards—those, for example, with an institution as an author or a card for a special series of books. Each library has its own unique character. Take the time to know your library and if you can't find something or do not understand a card reference, ask the librarian.

Remember that modern libraries have much "non-book" material available. Pamphlets and clippings are kept in what are known as "vertical files." Record albums and films may be borrowed from some libraries. Many libraries have special programs for book discussions and some libraries offer books in braille and "talking books" (books on records or tapes) for the blind. Libraries today are not just storage places for books. They are a vital source not only of information but also of entertainment.

TERMS USED IN REFERENCE MATERIALS

APPENDIX (plural APPENDIXES or APPENDICES)—Additional material following the main text of a book. The material is usually supplementary and not essential to the book. Appendixes often contain the complete texts of documents and statistical information.

BIBLIOGRAPHY—A list of books and articles by an author or about a particular subject (or it can be a list of books published in a country, in certain languages, etc.). In a reference book the bibliography usually is a list of sources which serves to indicate the references the author used in writing his book or article and it also serves as a guide for the reader to additional information on the subject.

CONCORDANCE—An alphabetical index of the principal words of a book (such as the Bible) shown in context and with a reference to the passages in which they occur.

COPYRIGHT—Usually the back of the title page contains the copyright date. Books published after Sept. 15, 1955 have the symbol ©, which protects copyright holders. It is the exclusive right, granted by law for a certain number of years, to control copies of a literary, musical or artistic work. Sometimes a frequently revised book will show a copyright date for each revision. Additional "printings" may be listed here, but the latest copyright date shown is the year the book was first printed in its present form. (The copyright date is not always the same as the publication date—see TITLE PAGE definition.)

CROSS REFERENCES—There are two kinds of cross references: "see" references and "see also" references. A *see reference* directs the reader from a heading not used to the one used by the author. (For example: "Farming see Agriculture.") A *see also reference* is one which gives pages for the heading checked and then refers the reader to related topics. (For example: Latin

America see also Alliance for Progress.) Some indexes put the page references under all headings rather than use cross references. And unfortunately some indexes have no cross references and do not put the references under various possible headings so the reader must search his vocabulary for synonyms to determine the subject heading used.

GLOSSARY—An explanation of the vocabulary used in the book— especially in books using foreign or scientific terms which need definition. (This list of terms that you are reading is a glossary.)

INDEX—The index to a book (or to a set of books) is an alphabetical list of people, places and office topics mentioned in the text. After each entry the numbers of the pertinent page or pages are given (or the volume number and pages if the index is to a set of books).

INTRODUCTION, PREFACE AND FOREWORD are terms often used interchangeably. They refer to the sections in the front of the book which give a brief statement about the book by the author (or another person) and contain acknowledgment of the assistance of others and suggestions by the author to the reader about the material.

GAZETTEER—A geographical dictionary giving names and descriptions of places.

TEXT—The main part or body of a book.

TITLE PAGE—The page at the front of the book with much important information. It gives the full title, the name of the author and sometimes his degrees, etc., the name of the publisher, and the place and date of publication. (Note: the publication date may be different from the copyright date, which usually appears on the back of the title page.)

VERTICAL FILE—Pamphlets, clippings and other materials which are not suitable for classification and a place on the library shelf are often filed in an "information file" or "vertical file" (because the items are filed standing on edge). Such material is given a subject heading, placed in a folder with that same heading and then filed in deep-drawer cabinets.

ABBREVIATIONS USED IN REFERENCE MATERIALS

anon.—anonymous
c—copyright
cf.—confer; or compare
ch.—chapter
col., cols.—column, columns
comp.—compiler
cm.—centimeters (the size of the book as shown on the catalog card)
diagrs.—diagrams
ed.—editor, edition, edited
e.g.—*exempli gratia;* for example
enl. or enlar.—enlarged (material added)
et al—and others
et seq.—*et sequens;* and following
f., ff.—page or pages following
fac.—facsimile
fig., figs.—figure, figures
ibid.—*ibidem;* the same reference as the one immediately preceding
id.—*idem;* in the same place
i.e.—*id est;* that is
illus.—illustrator, illustrated, illustration
incl.—including
loc. cit.—*loco citato;* the same passage as that just cited by the author whose name is given.
mounted pl.—mounted plates; full-page illustrations
ms., mss.—manuscript, manuscripts
op. cit.—*opere citato;* the same work as the one previously cited by the author whose name is given.
p., pp.—page, pages
passim—here and there
pseud.—pseudonym

q.v.—*quod vide;* which see   qq.v.—plural "which see" (a see reference to more than one other heading)

recto—right-hand page of a book

rev.—revised (the material has been changed and brought up to date)

sec., secs.—section, sections

[sic] for "thus," bracketed and used to indicate that the preceding error is to be found in the original source

tr.—translator, translation

verso—left-hand page of a book

viz.—*videlicet;* namely

v. or vol., vols.—volume or volumes

FOOTNOTES AND BIBLIOGRAPHY

A footnote is an explanatory or bibliographic comment or note at the bottom of a page.

An explanatory footnote is used to free the text of incidental material and still amplify the discussion for the reader who might be interested. The following explanatory footnote was indicated in *The Modern Researcher* in a discussion of the Mohammedan and Christian calendars:

> 2 The Moslem year is computed from the Hejira, or Flight of Mohammed, in A.D. 622. Since it is a lunar year, it is shorter than ours, and this accounts for the fact that 622 plus 1156 equals more than 1743.[1]

In the writing of any paper many ideas and facts are borrowed from others and the use of bibliographic footnotes enables the writer to give recognition to important sources and to establish the validity of a statement. If footnotes are not used the borrowed idea or fact becomes stolen. Honesty is the scholarly policy. After the first reference to a work has been cited in

---

[1]Jacques Barzun and Henry F. Graff, *The Modern Researcher* (New York: Harcourt, Brace, 1957), p. 116.

full, *Ibid.* (Latin, *Ibidem,* in the same place) may be used but only when the next reference is to the same work with no other work intervening.

¹Lewis S. Feuer, *The Conflict of Generations; The Character and Significance of Student Movements* (New York: Basic Books, 1969), p. 11.
²*Ibid.,* p. 41.

If there is a second reference to a work already cited in full but with other references intervening, *op. cit.* (Latin, *opere citato,* in the work cited) is used with the author's name.

¹Lewis S. Feuer, *The Conflict of Generations; The Character and Significance of Student Movements* (New York: Basic Books, 1969), p. 11.
²Dorothy Day, *The Long Loneliness* (New York: Harper, 1952), p. 39.
³Feuer, *op. cit.,* p. 50,

Or instead of *op. cit.* the author's name and a shortened title may be used: Feuer, *The Conflict of Generations,* p. 17.

If more than one work by the same author has been cited in the footnotes, then the title of the work would also have to be included in subsequent footnotes to make the reference clear:

¹Martin Luther King, Jr., *The Trumpet of Conscience* (New York: Harper & Row, 1968), p. 70.
²Martin Luther King, Jr., *Where Do We Go From Here; Chaos or Community?* (New York: Harper & Row, 1967), p. 35.
³King, *Trumpet of Conscience,* p. 99.
⁴King, *Where Do We Go From Here,* p. 50.

Each footnote is indicated by the number at the end of the statement to which it refers. Footnotes in a book may be numbered serially either on each page, or by chapters, or for the entire book. Footnotes may also be numbered and listed consecutively on a separate page at the end of a report or paper. The numbers calling attention to the footnotes are written slightly above the line and should not be enclosed in parentheses or followed by a period or any punctuation. The main body of a typed report or paper should be double-spaced but the footnotes should always be single-spaced.

BIBLIOGRAPHY

The bibliography is a list of every work cited in the text or in the footnotes plus other pertinent sources. A bibliography must include every work referred to in a report or paper but it may also include works which contributed to the writer's ideas or conclusions but were not cited in the text. Padded bibliographies are ridiculous and only reveal a mind that thinks quantity, not quality. Do not list every work consulted. List only those which made a real contribution to your paper.

The form of the bibliography differs from that of the footnotes. The list is arranged alphabetically by the author's last name, does not include parentheses, and periods, not commas, are used between each part of the entry. The author's last name is against the lefthand margin and any succeeding lines are indented three spaces. For magazine articles the inclusive pages of the article should be given and for newspaper articles the page on which it begins and pages on which it may be continued (separated by a comma, as in the sample headed "Newspaper" below).

BOOKS

One Author

Footnote:
¹Lewis S. Feuer, *The Conflict of Generations; The Character and Significance of Student Movements* (New York: Basic Books, 1969), p. 14.

Bibliography:
Feuer, Lewis S. *The Conflict of Generations; The Character and Significance of Student Movements.* New York: Basic Books, 1969.

Two Authors

Footnote:

[2]Charles Judah and George Winston Smith, *The Unchosen* (New York: Coward-McCann, 1962). p. 17.

Bibliography:

Judah, Charles and Smith, George Winston. *The Unchosen.* New York: Coward-McCann, 1962.

Three Authors

Footnote:

[3]Hans H. Landsberg, Leonard L. Fischman, and Joseph L. Fisher, *Resources in America's Future.* (Baltimore: Johns Hopkins Press, 1963), p 2.

Bibliography:

Landsberg, Hans H.; Fischman, Leonard L.; and Fisher, Joseph L. *Resources in America's Future.* Baltimore: Johns Hopkins Press, 1963.

More Than Three Authors

Footnote:

[4]James Westfall Thompson, *et al.* (or James Westfall Thompson, and others), *The Civilization of the Renaissance* (New York: Ungar, 1959), p. 69.

Bibliography:

Thompson, James Westfall; Rowley, George; Schevill, Ferdinand; and Sarton, George. *The Civilization of the Renaissance.* New York: Ungar, 1959.

Editor

Footnote:

[5]Herbert Mitgang, ed., *Lincoln as They Saw Him.* (New York: Rinehart, 1956), p. 3.

Bibliography:
Mitgang, Herbert, ed. *Lincoln as They Saw Him.* New York: Rinehart, 1956.

MAGAZINE

Footnote:
    [6]Kenneth L. Woodward, "Seances in Suburbia," *McCalls,* March, 1970, p. 70.
Bibliography:
Woodward, Kenneth L. "Seances in Suburbia." *McCalls,* March, 1970, pp. 70-71, 149-151.

NEWSPAPER

Footnote:
    [7]J. Anthony Lucas, "The Drug Scene: Dependence Grows," *New York Times,* January 8, 1968, p. 22.
Bibliography:
Lucas, J. Anthony. "The Drug Scene: Dependence Grows." *New York Times,* January 8, 1968, pp. 1, 22.

ENCYCLOPEDIA

Footnote:
    [8]Harold E. Driver, "Indian, American," *Encyclopedia Americana,* 1969, XV, 27.
Bibliography:
Driver, Harold E. "Indian, American." Encyclopedia Americana. 1969. Vol. XV.

ENCYCLOPEDIA *(Unsigned Article)*

Footnote:
    [9]"Ironwood," *Encyclopedia Americana,* 1969, XV, 467.
Bibliography:
"Ironwood." *Encyclopedia Americana.* 1969. Vol. XV.

A FEW WORDS ON WRITING A PAPER

I⊤ is infinitely more interesting to you—and to your teacher—*if you gather facts in order to draw conclusions and present ideas* rather than simply to repeat facts. Fact collecting requires little thought and no decision. But the fact that Franklin D. Roosevelt became President in 1933 and the fact that the United States was in the midst of an economic depression in 1933 can be combined to form opinions on the logic of his administration's concern with social welfare and a "New Deal."

Develop an awareness of the reference book you're using. What is the publication date? Is it out of date? Does it matter? (A book about the origin of Halloween may have accurate, complete information even if it is old. Something on outer space or science might need to be very recent.) Who is the author? Does he have a particular bias? Does it matter? Should you search for an opposite opinion? (A book about automobiles written by an automobile manufacturer would have a totally different approach from one written by Ralph Nader, a critic of the industry's safety standards.) You might also remember that you may have a bias of your own which you bring to whatever you read. Bias or opinion is not, by the way, necessarily "bad" but it should always be taken into account when attempting to make impartial judgments. Finally, books are man-made, so even the best reference source may have some errors. So don't necessarily believe everything you read, and if you notice a discrepancy check further.

Though it may seem like wasting time, it usually saves time if you *read any "How to use this book" information and if you at least skim the introductory material.* This will give you an idea of the scope and aim of a book and may tell you immediately if it is of use to you. (Obviously, a U.S. history book covering only the colonial period is of no use to anyone studying the Civil War. The point is, the limits of a book may not be indicated in its title.)

Notice the wording and style of the source if you're reading something beyond straight factual information. "Louisa May Alcott wrote *Little Women*" is a fact. "Louisa May Alcott wrote that great classic *Little Women*" is not only an opinion but probably the beginning of an argument.

Make careful notes—preferably on cards, using only one side of the card or notepaper (or at least one idea to a card) so that you can later shuffle them to an order which is best when writing your paper. For any note taken be sure to include the exact citation to the source for use in a bibliography or footnote or to double check something you later question.

No attempt is made here to deal with the complex subject of writing beyond this reminder: *keep your writing clear and straightforward.* Be accurate and honest. Somewhere in the first paragraph or beginning of the paper make a concise statement of your subject and what the reader can expect from your paper; follow this with some orderly progression of the material (perhaps chronologically, perhaps by subject—for example, U.S. history by the date of events or by topics like government, economics, social history), and conclude the paper with a summary of ideas. It is recommended that you make an outline before you start to write but if you are the sort of person who gets hung up on such a procedure forget it and use whatever method is comfortable.

If you have even the tiniest amount of natural curiosity, the researching of a subject will lead to an interest in it, so don't resist the task. Keep an open mind, try to have a genuine involvement with the topic (even if it's assigned and not your choice) and the resulting attitude will allow you to *develop enthusiasm, deal creatively with the material* and give free play to your imagination.

SAMPLE TERM PAPER SHOWING
THE USE OF REFERENCE BOOKS

The following paper is an example of how to use the information found in reference books. It is an oversimplification meant only to illustrate the use of sources.

<u>OUTLINE</u>

Paper On Non-Violence

I.   Introduction and Purpose

II.   Definition of Non-Violence
      <u>Satyagraha</u> translations

III.   Some Practitioners of Non-Violence
      Jews, early Christians, Godwin,
      Shelley, Thoreau, Tolstoi, Gandhi,
      Martin Luther King, Jr.

IV.   Visible Reasons for Resorting to Violence
      Definition of violence
      Deprivation and poverty, frustration,
      slow process of government, brutality

V.   Invisible Reasons for Violence -
      (Psychological)
      Fear, Conscience, Attitudes
      Treatment of persons as things

VI.   Violence Harms Self as well as Others

VII.   Persuading the Enemy
      Gandhi's philosophy
      Understanding others
      Treating persons as humans

VIII.   Non-Violence as Action

IX.   Conclusion

<u>Remember</u> <u>When</u> <u>Mace</u> <u>Was</u> <u>A</u> <u>Spice</u> <u>In</u> <u>Mother's</u> <u>Kitchen</u>

Non-violence. It sounds like a recommendation to
not do anything, doesn't it? Or worse, it sounds like
consent to evil, or withdrawal. Maybe the "non" started
as a sly, semantic trick perpetrated by the violent as
a subtle put down. In any case, it is a philosophy that
is currently out of favor. Violence is in.

The purpose of this paper is to redefine non-violence
as an action. This is not a comprehensive study of the
philosophy. The hope here is to serve as a catalyst for
a consideration of non-violence as a positive force and
to argue that violence is a negative force whose chief
reality is self-destruction.

The paragraph above is a
statement of the theme.

The message of <u>satyagraha</u> has been diluted and confused in the passage from Gandhi's word to our word, non-
violence. <u>Satyagraha</u> has been more correctly translated
as "strength of truth," "force of soul," "steadfastness
for truth," "grasp of truth," "truth force," and "creative
force." These stronger definitions better represent the
two principles in the practice of <u>satyagraha</u> -- to adhere
to the truth and to defend it to the utmost by voluntary
suffering. It is in these stronger terms that the word
non-violence is used in this paper.

As an extreme opposite of violence, non-violence implies the same force as violence but it is transformed into a moral force. The non-violent seek not to destroy the enemy but to convert him. Gandhi is quoted: "I seek entirely to blunt the edge of the tyrant's sword, not by putting up against it a sharper-edged weapon, but by disappointing his expectation that I would be offering physical resistance."[1]

Found through the Reader's Guide to Periodical Literature under the heading "nonviolence."

NONFERROUS metals. See Metals, Nonferrous
NONSENSE verse
    See also
  Mother Goose
NONVIOLENCE
  Gandhi: the heritage of non-violence; sym-
    posium. UNESCO Courier 22:4-32 O '69
  What role for non-violence today? excerpts
    from Gandhi's truth. E. H. Erikson. Cur
    112:42-7 N '69
NON-WAGE payments
  NRPA's personal security program; includ-
    ing life insurance benefits. D. D. Magee.
    il Parks & Rec 4:73-4 S '69
NOONAN, Joseph
  Something new. Cath World 210:73-9 N '69

The idea of non-violence is an ancient concept though it did not always have a name and was not always a clearly defined philosophy to those who practiced it.

In A.D. 37-41, the Jews are said to have practiced non-violence in resistence to Roman emperor Caligula's

1 René Habachi, "The Heritage of Non-Violence," UNESCO Courier, October, 1969, p. 13.

determination to force the Jews to erect his statue in the Temple at Jerusalem.[2] The Sermon on the Mount is usually considered a non-violent philosophy and early Christians refused to pay taxes to support heathen temples.[3]

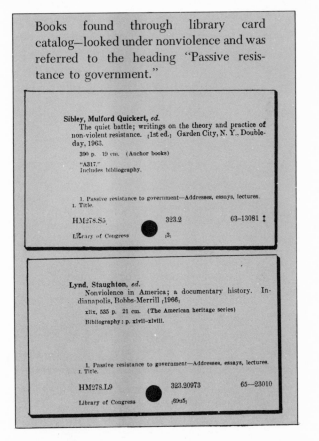

Books found through library card catalog—looked under nonviolence and was referred to the heading "Passive resistance to government."

Sibley, Mulford Quickert, *ed.*
The quiet battle; writings on the theory and practice of non-violent resistance. [1st ed.] Garden City, N. Y.. Doubleday, 1963.

390 p. 19 cm. (Anchor books)

"A317."
Includes bibliography.

1. Passive resistance to government—Addresses, essays, lectures.
I. Title.

HM278.S5   323.2   63–13081 ‡

Library of Congress   [3]

Lynd, Staughton, *ed.*
Nonviolence in America; a documentary history. Indianapolis, Bobbs-Merrill [1966]

xlix, 535 p. 21 cm. (The American heritage series)

Bibliography: p. xlvii–xlviii.

1. Passive resistance to government—Addresses, essays, lectures.
I. Title.

HM278.L9   323.20973   65—23010

Library of Congress   [69u5]

2 Mulford Q. Sibley (ed.), The Quiet Battle (Chicago: Quadrangle Books, 1963) pp. 111-115.

3 Staughton Lynd (ed.) Nonviolence in America: A Documentary History (New York: Bobbs-Merrill, 1966) p. 11.

The eighteenth century philosopher William Godwin in his <u>An Enquiry Concerning Political Justice</u> (1793) asserted that the best way to effect a revolution in any political system was to change through persuasion the opinion on which all government is founded. Godwin probably influenced his son-in-law Percy Bysshe Shelley, who wrote <u>The Masque Of Anarchy</u> after reading about peaceful demonstrators being fired upon by British troops.[4]

Early American history is filled with incidents of the use of non-violence, as in the life style of the Quakers[5] and in the life of Henry David Thoreau, who had

> Thoreau quotation from *The Oxford Companion to American Literature* and not footnoted because essay is famous and found in many sources.
>
> **Civil Disobedience,** essay by Thoreau (q.v.), originally delivered as a lecture, and first printed as 'Resistance to Civil Government' in Elizabeth Peabody's *Aesthetic Papers* (1849).
>
> Asserting that 'That government is best which governs not at all' and that 'Government is at best but an expedient,' the author points to such injustices and abuses as the prosecution of the Mexican War, the treatment of native Indians, and the institution of slavery. To co-operate with government, even to

4 Sibley, <u>op. cit.</u>, pp. 21-24
5 Lynd, <u>op. cit.</u>, pp. 3-21

refused to pay taxes and in his essay on civil disobedience states: "Under a government which imprisons
any unjustly, the true place for a just man is also in
prison." The essay later influenced Gandhi.[6]

> The *Reader's Encyclopedia* and footnoted
> because of claim to have influenced Gan-
> dhi.
>
> **Civil Disobedience** (1849). An essay by Henry
> David THOREAU. Its major premise is "that govern-
> ment is best which governs least." Thoreau asserts
> that a man's first loyalty is to his own nature; true
> to himself, he may then be true to a government. The
> essay influenced Gandhi's doctrine of passive resist-
> ance.

Three well known advocates of non-violence in
more recent times are Leo Tolstoi, Mohandas K. Gandhi
and Martin Luther King, Jr. The list, of course, is
much, much longer.

Even some historical figures commonly associated
with rebellion have spoken out against violence. The
theme of alienation is important to current theories
of non-violence. Albert Camus, writing of this psychological state, believed in a life committed to becoming
more humane and thereby more human and more alive as a
person. "For Camus, physical violence is the supreme
evil, but he does not rule out its use entirely; violence must be used only to reduce or forestall far more

        6 William Rose Benet, The Reader's Encyclopedia
(New York: Crowell, 1965) p. 202

worse violence in the immediate future, as a last,
desperate resort, if no nonviolent means are available."[7]

Using the index to the *International En-cyclopedia of the Social Sciences* the reader is referred to the heading "Civil Disobedience" among other headings. Note the "see also" reference to "violence."

Nonviolence
civil disobedience 2:473, 474, 478
community disorganization 3:167
Indian political thought 7:178
pacifism 11:353 fol.
race relations: world perspectives 13:275
see also Violence

Even Marx had a tempered view:

The more dubious and uncertain an instrument violence has become in international relations, the more it has gained in reputation and appeal in domestic affairs, specifically in the matter of revolution. The strong Marxist rhetoric of the New Left coincides with the steady growth of the entirely non-Marxian conviction, proclaimed by Mao Tse-tung, that "Power grows out of the barrel of a gun." To be sure, Marx was aware of the role of violence in history, but this role was to him secondary; not violence but the contradictions inherent in the old society brought about its end. The emergence of a new society was preceded, but not caused, by violent outbreaks, which he likened to the labor pangs that precede, but of course do not cause, the event of organic birth. In the same vein he regarded the state as an instrument of violence in the command of the ruling class; but the actual power of the ruling class did not consist of or rely on violence.[8]

7 Christian Bay, "Civil Disobedience," *International Encyclopedia of the Social Sciences*, ed. David L. Sills, (New York: Macmillan, 1968) vol. 2, pp. 478-479

8 Hannah Arendt, *On Violence* (New York: Harcourt Brace Jovanovich, Inc.) p. 11

The visible reasons for resorting to violence are many and dramatic. Violence is, of course, as old as its opposite. The <u>Oxford English Dictionary</u> uses two and one half pages to show the use of the word in its

> Because the writer is stating that violence is old and is then going on to define the word, the *Oxford English Dictionary* is used since it emphasizes the historical development of words.

various forms, going far back in time. The OED defines violence as the exercise of physical force so as to inflict injury on, or cause damage to persons or property...treatment or usage tending to cause bodily injury or forcibly interfering with personal freedom.

And there are subtler meanings which can only be hinted at here. There is, for example, the theory that secret thoughts can do violence or even that "haste is violent in the dimension of time. We have our own natural rhythms and we develop harmoniously and gently only if we conform to them."[9]

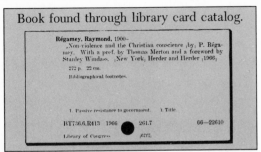

Book found through library card catalog.

Régamey, Raymond, 1900-
,Non-violence and the Christian conscience ,by, P. Réga-
mey. With a pref. by Thomas Merton and a foreword by
Stanley Windass. ,New York, Herder and Herder ,1966,

272 p. 22 cm.

Bibliographical footnotes.

1. Passive resistance to government. 1. Title.

BT736.6.R413 1966   261.7   66—22610

Library of Congress   ,6777,

9 Pie Régamey, O.P., <u>Non-Violence and the Christian Conscience</u> (New York: Herder and Herder, 1966) p. 169.

One of the chief visible reasons for violent action is poverty and deprivation. Collective violence is likely to occur in a nation in which most citizens feel deprived and feel they have exhausted constructive means available to them and lack nonviolent opportunities to act on their anger. The slow process of government, that unoiled, unwieldly machine that doesn't work fast enough, is another visible reason for violence. Government may not recognize a problem, or if it does there remains the gap between the recognition of need and the accomplishment of change. Violence is often used to call attention to a problem ignored and to goad those in power to change their attitude.

The situation is further complicated by the fact that non-violence sometimes begets violence. An insensitive, established power will sometimes not distinguish between peaceful and non-peaceful tactics. A sit-in is not the same as burning a bank. If a peaceful tactic brings brutal repression it tends to radicalize the non-violent movement.

The frequently vivid contrast between what is taught in schools and homes and the actual state of affairs in the world causes a frustration which leads to violence. And since short-term goals are often achieved by violence, this tends to reinforce such a pattern of behavior.

The belief that the end justifies the means is another factor of violence. The process of violence, like all action, changes the world, but the non-violent

SAMPLE TERM PAPER

believe that the most probable change through that
process is to a more violent world; the end is overwhelmed
by the means. The advocates of violence contend that
a period of temporary violence is necessary to accomplish
goals. The risk they face is that violence might become
a habit. As Hannah Arendt observed, even revolutionary
Frantz Fanon admitted that "'unmixed and total brutality,
if not immediately combatted, invariably leads to the
defeat of the movement within a few weeks.'"[10]

> Non-violence is not always the heading used, as seen in the catalog card headings. But the library catalog will refer the reader to the heading used—such as "Passive resistance to government."
>
> And, as indicated in some of these examples, it is useful to check under opposite headings ("violence") and related headings ("terrorism"). These will often be suggested in "see also" references.
>
> Other headings may be searched depending on the direction the material is taking ("colleges and universities" for campus disorders).

The accusation that violent behavior is easier in
the sense that it does not practice the disciplines of
love and does not restrain itself from the thing it
opposed in the first place -- the forced role under

10 Arendt, op. cit., p. 14 footnote

another's opinion -- calls for a look at the invisible reasons for violence.

The blunted conscience, the unacknowledged and unconscious conflicts which explode and generate wars, and fear which causes hate and killing are viewed as psychological reasons for violence.[11] Most important, warped attitudes leading to the treatment of persons as things are a large factor in violent behavior. Violence forces people to act in a way they would not freely choose and so it destroys them as persons. Violence produces resentments which work havoc on personality. Treating others as things allows the offender to kill them because they are not viewed as human. Without mutual recognition of humanity, no love is possible. Here is Robert Brustein, dean of the Yale School of Drama, writing in The New York Times:

> "The moral superiority of the peace movement is vitiated by those who urge us to 'bring the war home,' for they are asking us to become one with the very thing we oppose. We must beware of those who call others 'pigs,' just as we must beware of those who call others 'effete impudent snobs' -- both are dehumanizing the opposition in preparation for committing inhuman acts against it."[12]

If one believes, as the practitioners of nonviolence do, that every act which harms others harms the self as well, one must focus on the quality of life as it is lived as well as on intermediate goals.

11 Régamey, op. cit., 136-174

12 Robert Brustein, "Topics: A Matter Of Accountability," The New York Times, April 18, 1970, p. 28

Gambling — Dominican Republic, Ap 29
BRUSTEIN, Robert (Dean). See also Colls — US —
Student Activities, Ap 18. US — Pol — Fringe Pol
Movements, Ap 18 in Ap 18 par. US Armament —
Draft, Ap 18 in Ap 17 par
BRYAN, D Tennant. See also Associated Press, Ap 22

The reference to the quotation on the opposite pages can be found in the *New York Times Index*. Shown here is the author entry, which refers the reader to the subject headings under which the complete citation will be found. Also shown is the entry as it appears under one of the subject headings "Colleges and Universities— U.S.—Students' Activities and Conduct."

school and hs educ in urban areas as way of solving
open admissions problems without diluting acad
standards, Ap 26,IV,13:4
 ● *Research.* **See also** Science — US, Ap 23,30
 ● *State Aid.* **See** subhead US — Finances, Ap 17
 ● *Student Activities and Conduct.* **See also** Med —
NYC, Ap 19. NYC — Environmental Problems
(General), Ap 20,23. US — Environmental Problems
(General), Ap 20,21,23,24 in Ap 17 par
 Prof S W Page Jr on New Left on campus scores
faculty who participate in campus agitation, calling
them seducers of naive students whom they use in
quest of their power goals, Ap 17,36:3; Dean R
Brustein article says youthful radicals must be held
accountable for their actions and warns against
concept that idealistic goal justifies any behavior,
Ap 18,28:3; Calif Gov Reagan calls for 'blood bath' to
deal with campus demonstrators if necessary, s to pol

The journey, not the arrival, matters. Frequent resorts to violence continually lessen the distinction between when it is "necessary" and when it is not and violence risks becoming a way of life as casually donned as a garment:

> "So pride is their chain of honour,
> violence the garment that covers them,
> their spite oozes like fat,
> their hearts drip with slyness." Ps 73:6

Found through Cruden's *Complete Concordance to the Old and New Testament.*

Because violence is in disharmony with what is best in self it finally cuts itself off from humanity. In an article in The Times Magazine, Irving Howe said:

> "The life of the political terrorist is overwhelmed by loneliness, not merely because he can no longer trust completely friend or comrade, but because he cuts himself off from all movements and communities in which choices can be weighed. Staking everything on the act, he blocks off all that comes before it and all that comes after. Deciding whom to smite, he replaces God. Choosing whom to punish, he replaces the justice (be it good or bad) of society. And since the conflicts of social classes must be bent on his will, he replaces history, too. The terrorist carries a moral burden only saints or fanatics would undertake -- worst of all, fanatics mistaking themselves for saints."[13]

The *Reader's Guide* indexes the New York Times Magazine so this is found through that guide (violence has a see also reference to "terrorism"): and it is also found in the *New York Times Index*. Example of author entry from N.Y. Times Index 1970 which refers the reader to the subject headings under which the full citation will be given —"News—U.S.," and "U.S. Politics Fringe Political Movements."

---

13 Irving Howe, "Political Terrorism: Hysteria On The Left," <u>The New York Times Magazine</u>, April 12, 1970, p. 25.

A principal tactic of non-violence is persuading the opposition. This calls first of all for a recognition of the fact that the role of the doubter and the challenger is not the only one in the human drama. Therefore the role is not forced on anyone. Gandhi sought to convert, not force. His pervading mood was a spirit of giving the opponent the courage to change. The willingness to convert rather than to force is backed by a view of each person as human, not as thing. There is truth in the old cliche that one can best understand another by putting oneself in his place and proceeding from that insight. This point is made by the experience of a man who won the friendship of eagles and other wild animals and succeeded in getting a hen to snuggle down affectionately on the head of a fox. He said:

> "'I have no mysterious 'fluid'; quite simply
> I have always tried to put myself in the place
> of the animal I studied, and first of all to
> see how it looks upon the world that surrounds
> it...The universe has a very different meaning
> for each of them; it is not the same for the
> tortoise, the heron, the lizard, the eagle...
> To understand a given animal is to carefully
> reconstitute its universe, its way of living
> in order to perceive as closely as possible
> the significance to itself of what it does
> and expresses.'"[14]

Finally, non-violence is not passive, it cries for action. If you act contrary to justice and I remain silent, it is I who am unjust. We are guilty if we

14 Régamey, op. cit., p. 173.

whispered when we should have shouted. Many instinctive abdicators call themselves non-violent, a view which lacks an appreciation of peace as action. Even the peaceful Gandhi "believed in nonviolence, but also held that violence is better than cowardice."[15]

Non-violence as an active force is not easy. Martin Luther King, Jr. said: "A...point that characterizes nonviolent resistance is a willingness to accept suffering without retaliation, to accept blows from the opponent without striking back."[16] But given the "strength of

> Book found through card catalog under "King, Martin Luther" as a subject rather than as an author (subject cards behind author cards).

truth" it is possible for the action of non-violence to be, as Staughton Lynd says, "the vision of love as an agent for social change." Let us hope that Plutarch is right when he says: "Perseverance is more prevailing

15 Joan V. Bondurant, "Gandhi," The World Book Encyclopedia (Chicago: Field Enterprises, 1968) vol. 8, p. 25.

> *The World Book Encyclopedia* cited in footnote because claim that Gandhi held that violence is better than cowardice might be questioned.

16 Negro Heritage Library, A Martin Luther King Treasury (Yonkers, New York: Educational Heritage, 1964) p. 71.

than violence; and many things which cannot be overcome
when they are together, yield themselves up when taken
little by little." Non-violence claims to break the

Found in Bartlett's *Familiar Quotations* and not cited because easily found in most general quotation books. (The quotation is also indexed under "perseverance" and can be located in the Index to Authors under "Plutarch."

Viol of her memory, 955b
violet and vine, 642a
Viola, notes v. fiddles bass, 505a
Violate agreements, 972a
Violations, security against future
v., 426a
Violence, age of comfort and v.,
999b
and injury to humanity, 100a
and injury to willow, 100a
blown with restless v., 271b
covereth the mouth of the
wicked, 24a
dictatorship maintained by v.,
957b
nation at mercy of v., 1013a
never by v. constrained, 189a
not by force or v., 465b
overcome v. without v., 1082b
perseverance more prevailing
than v., 136b
truth not permit v., 897a
Violent and sudden usurpations,
480b
death of slaveholder, 684a
delights have violent ends, 224b
fear and danger of v. death,

circle of ever-increasing violence; it says that the
important thing is not the visible success of one's life
but its quality.

Our obligation here is to be truly alive, to learn
to love, whether this obligation is seen from a humanist
view, as a supernatural gift of God, or as a simple dic-
tate of conscience. It is difficult. There will be times
of failure.

That then is the plea. To be alive, active, and
non-violent. And if you aren't -- well, how would you
like a punch in the nose . . .

BIBLIOGRAPHY: TERM PAPER

Arendt, Hannah. *On Violence.* New York: Harcourt, Brace, Jovanovich, 1970.

Bay, Christian. "Civil Disobedience." *International Encyclopedia of the Social Sciences.* New York: Macmillan, 1968.

Brustein, Robert, "Topics: A Matter of Accountability." *The New York Times,* April 18, 1970, p. 28.

Cornell, Thomas C., and Forest, James, (eds.) *A Penny A Copy;* Readings from the Catholic Worker. New York: Macmillan, 1968.

Finn, James. *Protest: Pacifism and Politics.* New York: Random House, 1967.

Gurr, Ted Robert. *Why Men Rebel.* Princeton, N.J.: Princeton University Press, 1969.

Habachi, René. "The Heritage of Non-Violence." *UNESCO Courier,* October, 1969. pp 13-17.

Howe, Irving. "Political Terrorism: Hysteria on the Left." *The New York Times Magazine,* April 12, 1970. pp 25-27, 124-128.

Lynd, Staughton (ed.), *Nonviolence in America: A Documentary History.* New York: Bobbs-Merrill, 1966.

Negro Heritage Library. *A Martin Luther King Treasury.* Yonkers, New York: Education Heritage, 1964.

Regamey, Pie. *Non-Violence and the Christian Conscience.* New York: Herder and Herder, 1966.

Sibley, Mulford Q. (ed.) *The Quiet Battle.* Chicago: Quadrangle Books, 1963.

STUDY AND
COLLEGE AIDS   .

T HE *Student Weekly,* published by *The New York Times* for high schools, receives mail from students seeking advice. The *Student Weekly* prepared these three lists of books and pamphlets to answer some of the questions most frequently asked.

STUDY AIDS

How to Study by Harry Maddox. Fawcett Publications, Greenwich, Connecticut.

How to Study Better and Get Higher Marks by Eugene Ehrlich, Thomas Y. Crowell Co., New York.

Study Successfully by Morris Ely Orchard, McGraw-Hill Book Company, New York.

Prepare for College Study by Norman Pedde, Readers Press, 282 York Street, New Haven, Connecticut.

Study is Hard Work by Wm. A. Armstrong, Harper and Brothers, New York.

How to Study by Lester and Alice Crow, Collier Books, New York.

Best Methods of Study by Samuel Smith, Louis Shores, Robert Britain, Barnes and Nobles, New York.

COLLEGE ADMISSION
(see also books under "Education" in this guide)
How to Get Into College—by Frank H. Bowles. New York. McGraw-Hill Book Company.

How to Get Into College and Stay There—by Esther E. Diamond. Chicago. Science Research Associates.

How to Prepare for College—by Abraham H. Lass. New York. Washington Square Press.

How to Visit Colleges—National Vocational Guidance Assn., Washington, D.C.

Complete Planning for College—by Sidney Sulkin. New York. Harper and Row Company

College Ahead—by Eugene S. Wilson and Charles A. Bucher, New York. Harcourt, Brace and World.

A *Handbook for Counsellors of College Bound Students*—by Association of College Admissions Counsellors, Evanston, Illinois.

FINANCIAL AID FOR EDUCATION

Need a Lift?—American Legion, Indianapolis, Indiana

Financial Assistance for College Students: Undergraduate—by Richard C. Mattingly, U.S. Government Printing Office, Washington, D.C.

How to Beat the High Cost of College—by Claire Cox, Bernard Geis Associates, New York.

How to Pay for Your Child's Education—by Sidney Margolius, Public Affairs Committee, New York.

Financial Aid for College: A Letter to Parents. College Entrance Examination Board, 475 Riverside Drive, New York. Free.

The Cost of Four Years of College. New York Life Insurance Co., New York.

Facing Facts about College Costs. Prudential Insurance Co., Newark, N.J.

Financing an Undergraduate Education—by John H. Russell, U.S. Department of Health, Education and Welfare, Washington, D.C.

Your College Education—How to Pay for It—by Sarah Splaver, Julian Messner. New York.

SELECTED BIBLIOGRAPHY

Andriot, John L. *Guide to U.S. Government Statistics.* 3rd ed. Arlington, Va.: Documents Index, 1961.

Barton, Mary N. and Bell, Marion V., eds. *Reference Books; A brief guide for students and other users of the library.* 6th ed. Baltimore: Enoch Pratt Free Library.

Barzun, Jacques and Graff, Henry F. *The Modern Researcher.* New York: Harcourt, Brace, 1957.

Chamberlin, Mary. *Guide to Art Reference Books.* Chicago: American Library Association, 1959.

Courtney, Winifred, F., ed. *The Reader's Adviser; A guide to the best in literature.* 11th ed. New York: Bowker, 1968. 2 vols.

Gates, Jean Key. *Guide to the Use of Books and Libraries.* 2nd ed. New York: McGraw-Hill, 1969.

Jackson, Ellen. *Subject Guide to Major United States Government Publications.* Chicago: American Library Association, 1968.

Reference Books for Small and Medium Sized Public Libraries. Compiled by the American Library Assoc., Reference Service Division, Basic Reference Books Committee, Mary C. Barter, Chairman. Chicago: Am. Library Association, 1969.

Schmeckebier, Laurence F. and Eastin, Roy B. *Government Publications and Their Use.* Rev. ed. Washington, D.C.: Brookings, 1969.

Shores, Louis. *Basic Reference Sources.* Chicago: American Library Association, 1954.

Turabian, Kate L. *A Manual for Writers of Term Papers, Theses, and Dissertations.* 3rd rev. ed. Chicago: University of Chicago Press, 1967.

Walsh, S. Padraig, comp. *General Encyclopedias in Print.* New York: Bowker, 1969.

Wasserman, Paul and others. *Statistics Sources.* 2nd ed. Detroit: Gale, 1965.

Winchell, Constance M. *Guide to Reference Books.* 8th ed. Chicago: American Library Association, 1967. Supplement edited by Eugene P. Sheehy, 1968.

INDEX

MP11A